The Photographic Guide to
Jumping

Lesley Bayley
and John Bowen

D&C
David and Charles

A DAVID & CHARLES BOOK

First published in the UK in 2005

Distributed in North America
by F&W Publications, Inc.
4700 East Galbraith Road
Cincinnati, OH 45236
1–800–289–0963

ISBN 0 7153 1930 2

Printed in China by SNP-Leefung
for David & Charles
Brunel House   Newton Abbot   Devon

ALL PHOTOGRAPHS BY BOB ATKINS
except p.22, btm left, David & Charles/Kit Houghton.

Commissioning Editor: Jane Trollope
Art Editor: Sue Cleave
Desk Editor: Louise Crathorne
Project Editor: Jo Weeks
Production Controller: Jennifer Campbell

Visit our website at www.davidandcharles.co.uk

David & Charles books are available from all good
bookshops; alternatively you can contact our
Orderline on (0)1626 334555 or write to us at
FREEPOST EX2110, David & Charles Direct, Newton
Abbot, TQ12 4ZZ (no stamp required UK mainland).

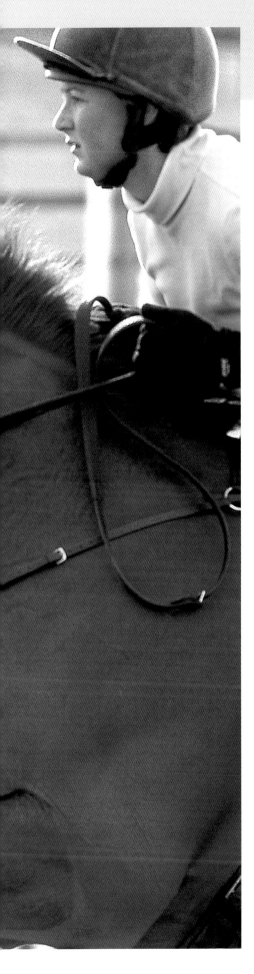

Contents

Introduction

For an exhilarating experience there is nothing like jumping a willing horse over a big fence. It's not only fun to do, it's great to watch – no matter what the discipline, the sight of horse and rider in flight is fantastic.

Whatever your interest, there are four basic types of jumping:

Show jumping – in an arena, usually over coloured poles but can also be over rustic or non-coloured poles or more 'natural' fences (such as the walls and banks seen in the famous Hickstead Derby). Show jumpers also jump water fences. All show jumps fall down if a horse hits them.

Cross-country jumping – generally speaking cross-country fences will not fall down if a horse hits them. However, recent safety measures mean some fences are now on frangible pins, which will allow the fence to fall under the weight of a horse in the case of what would have been a rotational fall. Cross-country courses make use of natural obstacles, such as hedges, banks and streams, and the fences are sited to make constructive use of the natural terrain. A cross-country course may be as much as four miles long. Cross-country jumping can be the only element in a competition, such as in hunter trials or team chasing, or it can be one phase in a competition, such as in a horse trial or a combined training competition.

Working hunter classes – in these classes, horses are required to jump around a course of more natural-looking fences that will knock down. The jumps are contained within an arena and may include doubles, spreads and uprights, much as you would find in a show-jumping arena. The fences differ in that the poles are rustic, though white poles or a white gate or stile may be included. Brush fences are also often used. Working hunter classes are show classes, intended to demonstrate a horse's performance and suitability as a hunter, as well as reveal his conformation and movement.

JumpCross – combines elements of show jumping and cross country. The courses extend over fields, making use of natural terrain and elements such as streams. However, the fences consist of coloured poles that will knock down. JumpCross is also an excellent introduction to cross-country riding, without the pressure of having to jump fixed fences. Riders can learn about pace, rhythm and balance, which are important elements in cross-country riding, but if they make a mistake, the fences will fall down.

This book covers jumping fixed and knock-down fences, with plenty of tips and exercises to help you become more proficient. However, before you even think about leaving the ground there is essential work to be done. For a horse and rider to consistently jump well a good deal of hard graft is needed. And this means regular practice, both on the flat and over fences. Use this book to provide ideas and exercises to develop your horse's jumping ability as well as improve your own technique.

JOHN BOWEN

John evented internationally and has ridden dressage up to Grand Prix level. Twenty years ago he started training students in all three disciplines – dressage, cross country and show jumping. Riders he has taught have achieved individual and team medals at Junior, Young Rider and Senior championships in eventing, and in dressage have represented their country at international Grand Prix level. Among his students is event rider Jeanette Brakewell. She has trained with him for the last 10 years and has won two Olympic team silver medals, three European Championship team gold medals and was individual silver medallist at the 2002 World Equestrian Games.

John is adamant that training is developmental and follows the correct stages. The system he uses encourages correct physical and mental development of the horse and rider partnership, establishing the correct basics at each level before progressing to the next. He works on balance, rhythm, suppleness, straightness, energy and the correct balance and position of the rider. His aim is for horse and rider to work together, forwards, in harmony.

Arena jumping

All jumping successes rely on certain principles that underpin the training of horses. No matter what kind of jumping you want to do, both you and your horse need to use these principles to acquire particular skills so that you can enjoy jumping – and be safe and do well. Before a horse can learn to jump he (and the rider) needs to have reached a good standard of education on the flat. Without a solid foundation, achieved through consistent and progressive schooling, neither horse nor rider will be able to jump well. For example, a jump is an exaggerated canter stride so the better – more powerful and balanced – your horse's canter, the better his jumping can be, and one of the keys to a powerful canter is schooling. In addition, to achieve a good flying change, which is often required when jumping a course, a horse has to be well schooled to develop his musculature and improve his suppleness, as well as to learn to respond quickly to your aids.

The importance of flatwork

All horses need regular flatwork as a key part of their preparation for jumping. Success in the show-jumping arena, or around a cross-country course, comes not only from the rider's and horse's jumping ability but also from their skill at negotiating the course in between the fences. The rider's ability to keep the horse balanced and fluent around turns and to approach and depart from each fence in a controlled, balanced manner, has a huge effect on the jump itself. Such control and fluency can only be achieved if the horse has a solid foundation of work on the flat.

Through schooling, all the physical requirements a horse must have for jumping – balance, suppleness, rhythm and impulsion – will develop. As his flatwork continues, his muscles will become stronger and

• Flatwork sessions that involve working your horse on the bit will develop musculature and allow him to carry himself and you efficiently.

• Use plenty of transitions to increase your horse's suppleness from poll to tail and ensure he is responsive to your aids.

• Working a horse like this, in a deep frame but moving actively forwards, stretching his neck down to take the contact, with his back raised and his hindlegs coming under his body, warms and loosens the muscles over his neck and back so that he is prepared for work.

his overall frame will change as he is taught to use himself efficiently and effectively. This not only leads to a horse that is more capable of jumping well, but also helps him to avoid injury and will prolong his working life. In addition, flatwork skills come into play around a jumping course. Transitions, for example, help soften a horse and encourage him to become rounder as well as improving his responsiveness to the aids. Turns on the forehand and haunches help the rider co-ordinate their aids and gain control over both ends of the horse so enabling them to ride better turns. As an instructor once said, at the start of a jumping lesson, 'Now we're going to do dressage with jumps.'

• You can see that this horse is starting to become a little strung out in his frame, tending to fall on to the forehand around a turn. This can happen as horse and rider progress around a course of fences – the riding time in between fences is just as crucial to the success of the jumping round as the jumping efforts. To keep a horse more upright on the turns use your inside leg.

FLATWORK SKILLS REQUIRED FOR JUMPING

The horse:

- needs to be responsive to the rider's aids – he must go forward willingly when asked, maintain the requested pace or movement until the rider says otherwise, stop when asked and be able to make changes of direction and pace.

- should be able to maintain rhythm, balance and impulsion so he can walk, trot and canter on both reins, executing turns, transitions and other exercises such as circles and serpentines easily. This necessitates the rider working to increase the horse's suppleness both longitudinally (from poll to tail) and laterally (from side to side).

- must be able to lengthen and shorten his stride when asked to by the rider.

- should be able to perform flying changes or change the lead easily through trot.

- needs to be working calmly and consistently before any jumping exercises are undertaken.

- must be supple and relaxed prior to jumping. Jumping a tense horse leads to resistance and the development of problems that need not be there! At worst, it can also result in injury, such as pulled muscles or ligament or tendon damage.

The rider:

- needs to be capable of communicating clearly with the horse to ask for all the schooling movements and exercises and must be able to ride them correctly, while staying in balance with the horse and having an independent seat.

- must learn to control the horse's shoulders and hindquarters so she or he can control the line of approach to the fence and execute good turns.

- must have the discipline required to go through exercises, calmly repeating them when necessary, to encourage the horse to work consistently, in balance and rhythm.

• Comparatively simple exercises, like trotting over a pole, have the potential to turn into an argument.

• Exercises on the flat can be used to get a horse concentrating on his work and help settle a lively horse that has excess energy. Don't jump an unsettled horse.

• By riding consistently but fairly and firmly, the rider overcomes the horse's initial objections and is soon jumping bigger fences without problems.

LINE OF SIGHT

A phrase you will come across a great deal throughout this book is 'line of sight'. Most riders are familiar with the saying 'where you look is where you go'. And it is really true – it could well be into the bottom of the fence if that is where we are looking! However, many instructors fail to expand on this and explain the influence of where the rider is looking upon his or her balance. As you will see from some photographs in this book, maintaining a correct line of sight can keep you safe and secure in the saddle, despite the occasionally alarming things happening to the horse underneath you.

Responsibilities

In order to jump well, horse and rider need to take on particular responsibilities: it is the rider's responsibility to get the horse to the fence on a good line of approach, in good balance and with the right amount of impulsion. It is the horse's responsibility to jump the fence. Remember that you have to be clear in your own mind that you intend to jump the fence, if you are at all doubtful the horse will sense this and will not jump as well or may stop. Clear communication from the rider is essential at all times.

Confidence and fitness

There are several other requirements in a good jumper. Confidence is a prized attribute – and for the horse this comes from being well prepared for jumping. He should never be overfaced but always have his ability developed progressively so that he comes to regard being asked to tackle a different fence – water, a drop or an arrowhead – as simply another obstacle that he can easily deal with.

Rider confidence is also vital – it is very easy to lose faith in your riding if you have a bad fall or ask too much of yourself before you are ready. Consistent and progressive training is just as essential for you as for your horse. Seek instruction, both on the flat and over fences, from a trainer you can trust.

Remember that your balance, suppleness, speed of reaction, fitness level and position play an important part in your success. A horse can be severely disadvantaged when jumping if the rider is always out of balance and landing heavily on his back or pulling on his mouth. Regular riding and working through grids will help your reactions and balance. Maintaining a good riding position means being aware of your posture and working at it every time you ride – self-discipline is needed here! Have regular lessons, but make use of photographs and video footage to analyse and work on your riding strengths and weaknesses.

How a horse jumps

Whatever the level of a horse's jumping experience, there are certain things that have to happen for him to negotiate a fence. These are physical adjustments of the horse's body that he makes but which the rider must allow for.

For example, the horse has to lower and stretch his neck as he jumps, so the rider's contact has to be elastic in order that she does not restrict the horse's movement.

• **Approach** As the mare approaches the fence she has to see it and work out what she needs to do. Bear in mind that the horse's vision is such that she has a blind spot directly in front of her nose, so the closer she gets to an object, the less of it she can see. By the time she takes off, she will have lost sight of the fence and is relying on her memory, experience and trust in her rider. There is a saying about never interfering with a horse in the last three strides before a fence – none of us would dream of interfering with a human athlete as they started their run up to the high jump! In these last strides, the horse has to make the physical alterations necessary to be able to jump the fence. She has to lower and stretch her neck so that she can relax and lift her forehand and round her back while bringing her hindlegs under her body to provide the propulsive force.

• **Take off** The leading foreleg straightens to push the front end into the air, the horse's centre of gravity shifts backward as she raises her head and neck so enabling her forehand to come off the ground. The hindlegs come underneath the body to support the horse's weight and then provide the thrust to make her airborne.

• **Landing and departure**
As she lands, all the weight of the horse is taken on one forelimb, although the second forelimb lands very soon afterwards. The forelimbs move quickly out of the way to make room for the hindlimbs to land within a split second of each other. The first departure stride from a fence is usually the first stride of the approach to another fence so the rider needs to have the horse balanced and under control immediately.

Assessing jumping ability

Loose jumping

It is useful to see a horse jumping without a rider as this can give an indication of his natural jumping style and ability. Although all horses can jump, some have more inherent ability than others. For instance, when loose jumping an inexperienced horse, you might notice that he instinctively uses his shoulders well and tucks his forelegs neatly underneath him, or he might be quite lazy in front, dangling one or both forelegs. Watching your horse jumping without a rider will also enable you to spot particular habits such as a tendency to waver to one side, to rush or to back off, to be lazy in front and so on, and this will give you an indication of areas you might need to work on. Bear in mind that young or inexperienced horses may initially make mistakes which will disappear with maturity or training. However, many horses jump very well without a rider and never show the same talent under saddle. This is worth bearing in mind if you are considering buying a horse having only seen it loose jumped or jumped on the lunge.

BENEFITS OF LOOSE JUMPING

Loose jumping is a good way of letting a horse find his own stride and balance. It also enables you to watch his jumping technique. You can observe whether:

• he is bold or rather cautious.

• he learns from any mistakes.

• he consistently takes off from a reasonable point.

• he thrusts off from both hindlegs evenly.

• his back looks rounded and he makes a good round shape (bascule) over the fence.

• he canters away on the correct lead and in balance.

• Jumping exercises can be used to improve a horse's forehand and/or hindleg technique and the way he uses his back. All horses, whether naturally talented or not, will benefit from correct training. However, not every horse will have the confidence or gymnastic ability to jump large fences or difficult and physically demanding combinations of fences.

Jumping on the lunge

Jumping on the lunge can be used to address schooling issues, such as napping and lack of impulsion, and to rebuild confidence, following a fall or if a poor rider has been hampering a horse over jumps, for example.

The person lungeing the horse must be experienced and quick on their feet. They must give the horse the freedom to move and jump throughout all the phases of the jump. You must

• Start with a small fence that has a placing pole in front of the fence and a guide pole on the inside. The placing pole helps to activate the horse's hindlegs so that it is easier for him to use himself effectively. As you would when riding, keep the horse on the correct line of approach with sufficient impulsion (created by tactful use and positioning of the whip instead of your legs).

ensure that the lunge line cannot get caught around the fence and, as with any jumping, be careful not to overface the horse so do not try to lunge a horse over a big fence if he has not jumped that height before.

TIPS FOR LUNGEING OVER FENCES

• Before you start lungeing over fences get your horse used to being lunged over poles. This also gives you the opportunity to improve his co-ordination, rhythm and balance. Using poles, especially if they are raised off the ground slightly, encourages your horse to flex his joints more. You can lunge over poles placed on a circle, eg one or three in a row (two encourages the horse to jump them as if they were a ditch) with about 1.2–1.5m (4½–5ft) from pole centre to pole centre. As they are on a curve, the distance will be correct if the horse is lunged over the centre of the poles. The distance will be shorter if the horse moves slightly to the inside of the circle and longer if he moves to the outside of the circle. Poles can be raised off the ground, using blocks so that they do not roll if touched by a horse's hoof.

• When you start to lunge over fences, use a small fence at first, such as a small cross pole or upright.

• Increase the height of fences gradually, as you would with ridden work, to build a horse's confidence.

• Use placing poles to help put the horse at the correct point of take-off.

• Remember to keep the rein contact but without restricting the horse's head and neck movement.

• Do not use side reins because the horse must have the freedom of his head and neck to act as a balancing pole.

• Have a lunge whip ready to give encouragement, but do not over-use it as this will make the horse panic and rush.

How a rider jumps

When jumping, the rider's job, quite simply, is to get the horse to the fence in the best possible balance, rhythm and pace, while the horse remains relaxed and obedient. Once there, the rider must remain in balance on take-off, over the fence and on departure, without restricting the horse's natural movement. We saw earlier (pp.12–13) how a horse has to alter his body to jump a fence. This is made more difficult with the extra burden of a rider. If the rider is also poorly balanced and stiff, the horse is hindered even more, as he constantly has to make extra adjustments to accommodate the rider. Horses do adjust their bodies to deal with their riders' weaknesses and they do this on the flat as well as over fences. Imagine you are giving a child a piggy back – if the child constantly slips to one side you alter your posture to try to keep the child securely in place. The horse does the same. For instance, if the rider collapses down his left side, the horse will try to even up the weight distribution on his back by propping up the rider with his left side. This is one of the reasons why many horses develop muscular imbalances in their bodies.

It's clear that if a rider has an independent seat and is balanced and supple it's easier for the horse to jump. If, however, a horse has to deal with a rider who is not balanced, is constantly left behind the movement, and hangs on via the reins, it's a much more tiring and unpleasant experience.

• The rider maintains an upright position and has resisted the temptation to tip forward before take off. Her weight is evenly distributed down through her lower leg into the heel.

• As the horse pushes off the ground with her hindlegs, the rider maintains an elastic contact through the reins so that the mare can continue to use her head and neck freely while negotiating the fence. Keeping her legs still and secure, the rider brings her seat out of the saddle for the jump.

• As the mare takes off, the rider follows her movement with her upper body, maintaining her stability through a secure lower leg. Note how her hands have moved forward to allow the horse freedom of the head and neck.

• As the hindlimbs descend, the rider maintains a good line of sight which aids her balance and security. Keeping her head up also keeps her weight in line with the horse's centre of gravity. Had she looked down, she would be more likely to tip forward, adding extra weight on to the front of the horse and making it more difficult for the mare to lift her forehand. She has also remained central and balanced in the saddle, which means the horse hasn't had to waste energy trying to keep her in place.

Improving your jumping position

Preparatory work: practising the jumping position

A rider's position has huge effects on the horse during all stages of the jump. This is most obvious when approaching the fence, at take off, in flight and on landing but is also very important during the get away and in between the fences.

Exercises, first on the flat and then over poles, will help to develop your position by increasing your balance and, by encouraging a good, light seat, will

• This rider demonstrates a good, balanced position, with her weight evenly distributed into the stirrups and a light, consistent contact on the reins. Note her line of sight, which is forward and horizontal to the ground. The horse is in good balance, helped by the rider's balanced position.

• Being in front of the horse's movement can spoil the picture. You can see that the rider has less weight in her heels and her lower leg position is weaker. Her head and shoulders are also well in front of her and her horse's centre of gravity, and her rein contact is less consistent. As she is out of balance she has caused her horse to drop on to the forehand and become unbalanced, too.

• Two views of a balanced and correct position over trotting poles. The rider's weight is evenly distributed in both stirrups and she has a relaxed tall position in the centre of the horse. Ask someone to check your position – if you are sitting crooked it will have implications when you start jumping. Note the similarity in the rider's balance and position to that shown above left.

free up the horse's back. Practising the required balanced position over trotting or canter poles will further develop your balance and be a natural progression towards small fences.

• Being behind the horse's movement also results in problems. Here our rider adopts a position that is too upright and is very tense. The tension in the rider is transmitted to the horse – look at the stiff and uncomfortable topline of the horse in this photograph compared to the first photograph on the left. (See also pp.20–21.)

• It is as important to be able to ride in the same balance when going around a turn or on a circle as it is when riding a straight line. You should also be able to maintain the same balance when sitting or in a light jumping seat.

EXERCISE FOR IMPROVING STRAIGHTNESS

This exercise involves riding over a pole, then through two cones and over another pole. The cones give the rider something to ride between and maintain the line. Start off with the cones about 1.5m (5ft) apart and gradually reduce the distance as you become more proficient. Alternatively, create a lane with two parallel poles instead of the cones. This would be an easier exercise as the poles act as guides and keep you straight.

• The rider has started to lose the horse's straightness – the mare is falling through her left shoulder and the rider is leaning to the right. The pair may be wonky because the rider's aids on one side were stronger than another – riding this exercise makes you aware of how you are using your aids. The resulting loss of straightness and direction takes the horse and rider off the line of the exercise and around the cone (below).

• As a result, they approach the final part of the exercise – the second pole – crooked.

• Repeating the exercise, the rider keeps the horse more between her hand and leg, which ensures she is straighter. It helps to think of riding the horse in a tunnel created by your hands and legs; this enables you to make the necessary corrections. When riding through the cones, check that there is equal space on either side.

Common position faults

Most rider position faults are due to physical tension in their general riding and a lack of confidence about jumping. To canter to a fence, looking over the top of it while maintaining a good balance and rhythm and following the horse's movement takes total confidence. Lack of confidence leads to a faulty position which affects the horse's balance and makes it more difficult for him to do his job. Horses are very sensitive to their riders' movements, responding to the slightest shift in weight. When the rider is in control of their body they can use this sensitivity to their advantage. For example, they can shift their weight to start turning mid-air in a jump-off. However, if a rider cannot control their body they can upset their horse's balance and even cause falls. It takes time, effort and discipline to overcome positional faults and achieve a good jumping position.

LOOKING DOWN: Looking down on the approach to the fence makes the rider tip forward prematurely so she gets in front of the movement. This affects her throughout the sequence and as you can see, on landing she is out of balance with the horse, which will affect how she rides the next fence on the course. In the second photograph you can see how tipping forward has resulted in the rider dropping the rein contact.

BEHIND THE MOVEMENT: Here the rider's tight and upright position means that she gets left behind the movement of the horse as he jumps. She is therefore out of balance, which the horse also feels, resulting in tension – this is reflected in both horse and rider as they land over the fence.

• **How it should be done** This head-on shot gives a general impression of straightness and balance in the horse, with the rider's weight evenly distributed in both stirrups. By looking ahead, she also ensures that she has a good line of sight.

PROBLEM GALLERY

• As the rider is looking down the horse's left shoulder she has become crooked, resulting in horse and rider drifting to the left over the fence.

• Here our rider has locked her knee and elbow, become in front of the movement and tight throughout her body. The expression on the horse's face says it all!

• The rider has allowed her lower leg to drift back and her upper body to fall forward (left), making her position very insecure. This results in an uncomfortable landing for both her and the horse (below).

TIPS ON ACHIEVING A GOOD JUMPING POSITION

- Do not clamp your knee on to the saddle as this makes you pivot around the knee, allowing your upper body to swing forwards and the lower leg to swing back, all of which weakens your position. Instead keep your knee soft and with your weight in your heels, concentrate on keeping your lower leg on. Practise trotting and cantering around the arena in a light jumping seat. If you struggle it's because your balance needs improving. Hold on to a neckstrap to assist your balance while you practise.

- When you practise your jumping position on the flat, keep your lower leg underneath you with the stirrup leathers vertical (above). Close the angles at your hip, knee and ankle joints to help you find your point of balance.

- Invest in lunge lessons to improve your balance (below).

- Beware of over-folding when tackling small jumps. If you over-exaggerate the fold of the body, you become out of balance and place too much weight over the horse's forehand. In addition, your horse's shoulders will be hampered if your weight is too far forward.

- Comparatively, your head is a very heavy part of your body. Remember to keep your head up to assist your balance and that of your horse. Launching yourself forwards too soon, puts your head and upper body ahead of the horse's centre of balance and makes for an awkward jump (above).

- Sit quietly in balance when you jump. Do not move around in the saddle unnecessarily – any shift of weight by you will be felt by your horse and could throw him off balance.

- Use a neckstrap (right) if you are jumping a young or unpredictable horse. You can grab the neckstrap in an emergency to maintain your balance – this is preferable to hanging on to the reins if you get left behind and possibly damaging the horse's mouth.

CONTACT WITH THE REINS

How much contact should you have on the reins? This very much depends on the horse. Event rider Lorna Clarke was famous for riding around huge cross-country tracks with long loose reins, something that worked for her because of the way she trained and rode her horses. While some horses appreciate the freedom of a loose rein just before take-off, others need more positive guidance on the approach to the fence, perhaps because they have a tendency to run out, or because they need the confidence of a secure contact. However, all horses should be allowed the freedom of their head, neck and shoulders over the fence and on landing, so the rider must soften their hands and follow the horse's mouth without restriction to allow for this. The ability to soften can only come about through a secure independent seat. If the rider has to rely on the reins for balance, they cannot soften their hands. Ask your instructor to demonstrate correct contact and softening of the hand so you know how this feels to your horse and what you should be aiming at. Here, the instructor is showing the rider the even pressure/contact that should be maintained throughout the jump (right).

Warming up

It's important to prepare your horse properly for any activity, whether it's a hack, a dressage schooling session or jumping. Warming up before work and taking the time to cool down afterwards is essential for all athletes – and especially for horses as they have huge muscle bulk; they need time to loosen up these muscles before any demands are placed upon them. If the muscles are not properly cared for, problems such as strains are more likely to occur.

Warm-up is particularly important when your horse has come straight out of his stable. You also need to plan your warm-up and work procedure according to your individual horse and the weather. Older horses may be stiffer and need more time to stretch and loosen – using magnetic rugs or rugs incorporating the foil that marathon runners wrap around themselves at the end of a run, will help to improve blood flow. If the weather is cold then you may not want to spend too much time in walk with a horse that is usually rugged up; consider using an exercise rug to keep him warm during the early slow work. The rug can be removed when more exertion is required. If the weather is hot, you may want to reduce your work period or re-schedule it for a cooler part of the day. However, if your horse is competing regularly, bear in mind that he will have to compete in all weathers, so he needs to train under all conditions as well.

PREPARING TO JUMP

- Walk on a loose rein for 5–10 minutes (below). Use straight lines and curves rather than small circles, make plenty of changes of direction to get your horse listening to you.

- Take up a contact and work your horse in walk and trot to establish that he is forward going and straight in each pace. He should move off the leg when asked, in a good rhythm. Ask him to go forwards actively but allow him to take the rein down so that he is stretching his neck, raising his back and bringing his hindlegs underneath him. You want him to loosen the muscles in his neck and over his back so that he is able to work with the minimum risk of injury. Work in rising trot, not sitting.

- If you know that riding straight is an issue for you and your horse, incorporate some exercises to help. For example, set out parallel guide poles at X then ride down the centreline and halt square and straight within their confines. Another idea is to ride a half circle from M (or any other suitable marker) to the centreline and then incline back to the track, riding alongside poles laid in a straight line.

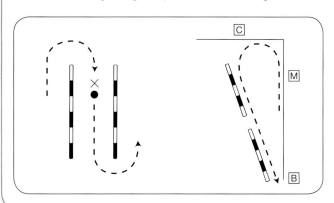

• Introduce canter (left) – adopt a forward seat with your weight out of the saddle to help the horse's back muscles. Make use of large circles and loops to test your horse's responses – the aim is to have him listening to you and doing as you ask, as soon as you ask it. Ask him to go on along the long side of the arena and then come back to you before the corner. Use transitions within a pace and from one pace to another to ensure he is responsive.

• As you warm up be aware of your position, and work through a mental checklist to ensure you are helping your horse as much as possible. If you are often told by your instructor to look up, remind yourself to look up when warming up your horse.

• Be aware of how your horse is reacting – if he is starting to get onward-bound then make use of circles and transitions (left) to steady him rather than allowing him to run on along straight lines. If your horse is getting tight in his neck and resistant, then flex him to one side and then the other to help soften him.

• Once you are warmed up, move on to the schooling you have planned to do, starting with something that your horse already knows, so that you give him confidence. Polework or gridwork is ideal. Then include some new work, perhaps a new grid or some dogleg turns, or practise jump-off techniques – whatever suits you and your horse.

• After completing a schooling or jumping session, you must allow your horse to cool down – trot him in a deep frame as you did when warming up to enable the muscles to stretch and loosen. Do this for a couple of minutes before moving forwards to walk and allowing him to walk on a loose rein until cool. Giving your horse's heart rate time to return to normal in this way, and allowing the muscles to cool down, will reduce the chance of him breaking into a sweat in the stable after work and having sore and stiff muscles the following day.

EQUIPMENT FOR JUMPING

It is just as important to protect yourself and your horse from injury when schooling as it is when competing.

- Ensure you wear an up-to-standard hard hat and proper footwear with a heel so that your foot cannot slip through the stirrup. I have seen someone who was dragged when his foot was jammed in the stirrup – it was not a pleasant sight. Make sure all your clothing fits well and is comfortable, both for practice and competing.

- Body protectors must be worn for cross-country jumping (see pages 86–7). Children should always wear body protection – and many adults are now also wearing protectors for show jumping and any jumping training.

- Gloves are a sensible precaution.

- You may also require a whip and/or spurs.

- Your horse should have a well-fitting saddle. Saddles specifically made for jumping are ideal – but there are many different variations and your saddle is very much a personal choice. However, it is absolutely essential that it fits the horse well – he cannot be expected to perform well if he is being cramped and is uncomfortable. Check the fitting regularly as horses can change shape quickly. You should also regularly check the stitching on the girth straps, your stirrup leathers and girth. You may choose to have stirrup irons that provide a springy feel – a good choice if you suffer from knee problems.

- Pay attention to your horse's bridle – in particular the browband should not be too tight or it will be a cause of irritation. Check the stitching carefully as breakages would be dangerous. Choose rubber-covered reins for increased grip – simple leather reins can become very slippery when wet.

- The choice of bit is dependent upon your horse – but please bear in mind that putting on a stronger bit does not necessarily solve the problem of a pulling horse. Sensible advice on bitting can be obtained from good tack shops and specialists selling bits via mail order.

- Breastplates and/or martingales may also be required.

- Protective boots for your horse are useful to prevent unnecessary knocks. There are several types of boots available, in various materials. In front use tendon boots (see photograph) and use brushing boots or fetlock boots behind, although speedicut boots also offer protection higher up the hindleg. Whether or not to use over-reach boots is a personal matter – some people feel a horse may tread on the boots, which would cause more problems.

• This rider is using a close-contact jumping saddle and has chosen front tendon boots and hind fetlock boots. She is also using a running martingale, attached to a breastplate. The bridle has a loose ring snaffle with a flash noseband, a combination that suits this particular horse. The rider also needs to be protected. Hats are available in various styles but must meet current safety standards, indicated on the labelling. While body protectors are essential for cross-country jumping, some riders like to use them when practising jumping at home, too.

Polework

Trotting poles

Both horses and riders tend to start their jumping careers by trotting over a pole on the ground. When a young horse is first presented with such a pole, his reaction can tell you about his character. He might react in a cool laid-back way and trot over calmly. Alternatively, he might stop, snort, go backwards and generally make a great fuss. Sometimes horses balloon over their first few poles, perhaps because they are suspicious, or maybe because they are enthusiastic. Whatever your horse's first reaction, careful repetition of the simple exercise of walking over a pole should increase his confidence and bring about an improvement. With repetition, even a very suspicious over-reactive horse should become calmer.

Poles can be used in many ways to educate and develop a horse and rider. The rider needs to think about guiding the horse over the poles in a good rhythm and balance. They should not allow the horse to rush or lose energy through the poles but should aim to keep the same impulsion and rhythm on the approach, through the poles and on departure.

Introduce novice horses to poles in their flatwork and lungeing sessions. Place poles randomly in the school so the horse learns to trot and then canter over single poles without fuss as part of his normal flatwork. When teaching young horses about jumping always have plenty of time so that if you hit a problem you can spend whatever time is needed to get round the difficulty without the event becoming stressful for all.

A novice rider should do polework on a horse that is a steady and confidence-giving jumper as they have enough to think about negotiating the poles without having to push on or hold back a horse. Exercises such as those described here are especially useful if you have a horse that tends to light up at the sight of poles and fences. Incorporating polework into his daily flatwork sessions will help accustom him to tackling poles calmly.

Poles in a row

These can be placed in several places including along one long side of the arena, along the centreline so that they can be approached from C or A, or across the school so that the approach is much shorter, from B or E, for example.

Start off with the easy option, that is along a long side of the arena. The arena fence will prevent the horse running out on that side so the job of riding him through the poles is easier for the rider. Set the distances between the poles according to your horse's stride length; as a rough guide start at 1.4m (4½ft) for a 16hh horse. Ideally, at trot, the horse should place his feet in the middle of the gap between each pole. If you need to adjust the distances do so gradually, shortening or lengthening by a couple of centimetres (1in) or so at a time, to find the ideal distance for your horse.

- Aim for the centre of the poles, approaching them in a rhythmical, well-balanced trot.

- Think about the turn before the approach to the poles. Plan ahead so that you get a well-balanced turn and remember that your horse may well lose impulsion on a turn, so ensure your leg is there, ready to be used to maintain the pace. Decide how much space to allow on the approach according to your horse's character. If he is onward-bound and 'buzzy', it might be beneficial to give him a fairly short turn into the poles or to ride them as part of a large circle.

- Tackle the poles on each rein, working equally from both sides. Aim for your horse to negotiate them calmly, without touching them, in a consistent rhythm.

- Do not overdo the polework. You risk boring your horse. This will lead to him being lazy, which defeats the object of the exercise.

- When you are both doing well over poles along the fence, try moving them onto the centreline. This way you can tackle them more quickly from either rein. For example, you could approach from the left rein, go over them and then change the rein so that your next approach is from the right rein.

GET CREATIVE!

Poles can be used in a number of ways – just use your imagination.

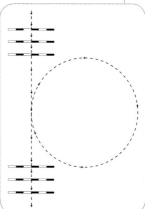

- Place two sets of three trotting poles leaving enough room between them to execute a 10-m (30-ft) circle off to the left or right or in the middle. This improves suppleness and ensures the horse is listening to you; it teaches rushing horses to wait for instructions. It helps you to improve your balance and rhythm.

- Put three poles across the school on the B-E line. This means you will need greater control, balance and rhythm as the turn to them will be very short, compared to the turn if they were along a long side. Make sure you can do the other exercises with poles before trying this arrangement. Once you can cope with three poles, ride a figure of eight with the poles in the middle of the 8. This will increase suppleness and encourage the horse to engage his hocks.

- Try basic school movements, such as serpentines and loops, with the addition of poles. For instance, ride over six poles and then turn to ride one or two loops of a serpentine by passing through the gaps between the poles. Do shallow or deep loops taking in a pole at various points along the loop. Or, space out the poles so that you can ride over a pole, execute a 10-m (30-ft) circle and then continue on to ride over another pole and so on. These exercises assist a horse's responses as well as improving his balance and suppleness.

- Another excellent exercise is to scatter poles at random around the arena. You can then decide to shorten your trot between certain points, or lengthen it from certain points, taking in the poles along the way. This helps to accustom the horse to tackle poles using different stride lengths and also tests your ability to stay in balance. For variety, you might like to add in other elements such as making a transition two strides after negotiating a pole.

Poles on a curve

Arranging trotting poles on a circle or around a corner creates more flexibility. Set the distance between the poles through their centres. You can then shorten the horse's stride by riding the poles towards the inside of the circle or corner. Alternatively, lengthen the stride and use the poles on the outside of the circle or corner, where the distance is slightly wider. Teaching a horse how to lengthen or shorten his stride while remaining in balance is vital for successful jumping, and the poles give him an easy, comparatively unstressful reason for doing so. As the rider, you will learn how to ask for and feel a change in stride length.

Raised poles

The exercises using trotting poles can also be done with raised poles. However, this is much harder work for the horse and you must consider this when compiling your horse's daily work schedule. Initially, the trotting poles would be raised on alternate ends and the horse trotted through from both reins. Both ends of the poles can then be raised – so each pole is just 5cm (2in) or so off the ground.

As a rider, you will notice the horse use himself more when trotting over raised poles; he has to flex his joints more to clear the poles and this makes him feel as if he has more lift in his trot. This extra flexion is very clear when you watch from the ground. There's a challenge to the rider, too: your seat and balance will be tested as your horse will feel much more springy – if you are slightly out of balance at the first pole you will feel more uncomfortable at the second pole and so on. A properly positioned, secure, lower leg will pay dividends, so if you find this exercise difficult, check your

lower leg. Is it swinging back as you trot along? Or is pushed too far forwards, sending your seat backwards? Improve your lower leg position by spending time trotting and cantering around in a light seat, concentrating on keeping the lower leg underneath you – if the position is good it should not make any difference to your stability if your horse was suddenly whipped out from underneath you. Working through raised poles helps your horse's attentiveness and engagement, balance and regularity of stride. Over time it will also assist in building his strength.

Canter poles

Cantering poles placed randomly around the arena teach horse and rider to keep the same balance and rhythm, irrespective of what they are going over on the ground. You can also practise turns and changes of direction over these poles to help you learn how to maintain rhythm and impulsion.

Try altering the layout of the canter poles to work on various aspects of your riding or your horse's way of going. For example, placing two poles in a line, say 14.5m (48ft) apart enables you to practise lengthening and shortening strides. For this distance you would expect to get four average length strides in between the two poles. Once you have achieved that, lengthen your horse's stride so that you are achieving three even strides. Then shorten the canter, aiming for five even strides.

This work may not be easy at first – it is a good idea to do stride lengthening and shortening exercises in your dressage training sessions as well, as this ability to move your horse 'up and down the gears' will be essential in your jumping. A careful balancing act is particularly vital when shortening the stride – it is easy to lose impulsion, which can result in refusals at fences. For this, it is important to make use of your body position to help collect your horse while still having enough leg on to maintain impulsion. Remember that when you increase or decrease the stride length, you must still maintain the balance, rhythm and impulsion otherwise, when it comes to jumping, your horse will find it difficult to negotiate a fence.

LINE OF SIGHT

Maintain your line of sight when riding polework exercises – if your head drops down, you'll place more weight on your horse's forehand making it difficult for him to use himself effectively.

• Horse and rider meet the pole on a good, rounded stride, with the hindlegs coming well underneath and therefore being able to provide plenty of lift.

• With flatter, poorer strides, the horse is much more strung out and you can see how she's unable to bring both hindlegs underneath to produce the impulsion she had in the first photograph.

• Sometimes horses make a big effort over poles, perhaps due to inexperience or enthusiasm. Repeat the exercise until they gain the confidence to do it calmly and correctly.

Working with grids

There are many elements that make up a horse's jump training: gridwork is just one tool in the trainer's kit. It can be used to improve a horse's technique, co-ordination, speed of reaction and balance. At the same time, working through the grids assists rider balance, position and reaction so horse and rider improvement go hand in hand

Some trainers make great use of gridwork, others incorporate it into a wider programme of work. John does not make extensive use of grids, particularly those that are ridden in straight lines. Instead, he prefers to take elements of realistic courses and teach people control, balance and co-ordination while tackling problems such as dog legs, related distances, fences off turns and so on. This section covers those grids that he finds most useful.

TIPS FOR USING GRIDS

• Treat each horse as an individual – not every exercise will benefit every horse. While repetition is necessary if a horse is to understand what is needed and become confident with the exercise, there may also be times when you have to abandon an exercise. For example, if your horse is getting worse rather than better, it could be that the particular exercise does not help his problem, so stop what you are doing and try something else.

• Remember to approach grids from both reins. Your horse will naturally find one rein easier but your aim is to make him equally adept on either rein.

• The distances given are a guide – you may need to alter them according to your horse's stride length.

Points to consider as your horse works through grids

How balanced is he?
Because a horse has to deal with a lot of fences in quick succession, balance problems are shown up by working with grids. This is where flatwork is so beneficial. If he has a solid background in flatwork, he will find it easy to maintain an even length of stride between combinations and he will be able to co-ordinate his limbs so that he can jump tidily. An unbalanced horse will tend to alter his stride length through the grid in order to cope. Take account of your horse's experience, too. Youngsters often make mistakes when jumping because their balance and co-ordination are not so highly developed. They may even appear to be careless, but this should disappear as they mature and develop. As a young horse's balance on the flat improves he will find the jumping easier – another reason why flatwork schooling is so important. Good lateral balance helps the horse in keeping straight to his fences so that he can start the grid jumping in the middle of the fence and maintain this line throughout.

Is he jumping straight?
If your horse consistently jumps towards the right or left, first examine your own position to see if you are encouraging him to do so. A lack of lateral balance could also be the problem (see above). Alternatively, it could be that you have created the problem by using strong rein aids to correct a tendency to drift, instead of improving the horse's balance or using aids, such as guide poles, to help him initially. Think about line of sight and keep looking forward to the next jump instead of focusing solely on the one you are about to jump.

How easy is he to control, especially on landing?

If you find that your horse runs on after landing (above), his balance is lacking and your control needs to be improved. It's a case of going back to improving straightness and control on the flat – any deficiencies here will be magnified once the horse is jumping.

What is his jumping technique like?

How does the horse actually get over the fence (see pp.12–13)? Does he really use his shoulders and lift his forehand well clear, tucking up his forelegs? Or does he dangle one or both forelegs? Does he look rounded in his back or is he jumping flat and hollow? How is he using his back end – is he neatly tucking up his hindlegs? Obviously the technique required for a show jumper is different to that required for a steeplechaser, so the horse's job, along with his natural technique, have to be considered. Through training and gymnastic exercises, a horse's technique can be improved – but trainer and rider also have to recognize when a horse has reached the limit of his ability and they should not push beyond this. Some horses naturally have more scope or have a naturally good jumping technique, others have to work harder to achieve the same level…each horse must be treated as an individual.

Am I giving the horse the best possible chance of successfully negotiating this fence?

From the rider's point of view this means being balanced, clear in your signals, having the horse in front of your leg and keeping your own line of sight correct. It also means having the grid set at a suitable distance for the particular horse, asking him questions for which he has been properly prepared, introducing him to new types and colours of jumps sensibly and progressively, and constantly monitoring his performance. Horses show that they are unhappy about what they are being asked to do through their behaviour, such as napping, bucking, refusing, running out. The purpose of any training session is to further the horse's education, understanding and confidence so you must plan sessions accordingly.

Simple grid

When introducing gridwork, start with a simple question and add to this, slowly developing the complexity of what you are asking of the horse. An excellent way to begin is with a trotting pole placed 2.5m (8½ft) before a small upright. (Use uprights in preference to cross poles until straightness is guaranteed – it is the rider's responsibility to keep the horse straight. John believes that a cross pole unfairly punishes an unstraight horse.) Trot and jump through this exercise two or three times, then add a landing pole 3m (10ft) from the upright.

Next, place a second upright 2.7m (9ft) from the landing pole. Again jump this a couple of times before adding to it.

Continue to develop the grid by adding a small parallel 6.4–7.3m (21–24ft) away from the second upright to give one non-jumping stride. Then add another small parallel, set at two non-jumping strides, or 10–11m (33–36ft). Adjust the distances depending on the horse's stride pattern – there is little benefit to be gained from making a small-striding horse struggle over longer distances. Remember that distances from trot are shorter than from canter and adjust accordingly.

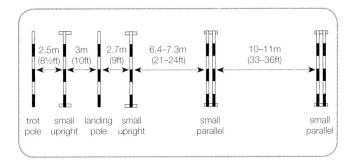

A bounce in

On your next session, start with the same grid, but then develop it to teach another lesson. For example, set a trotting pole 2.5m (8½ft) away from an upright, allow 3.6m (12ft) to another upright, then 6.4m (21ft) to another upright. This alteration means that you bounce in between the first two uprights (the horse does not take a stride in between these fences) and then have one stride before the final upright.

Using a bounce instead of a stride sharpens a horse's reflexes and can teach him to be a little neater in front. Start small so that you don't encourage him to hit the second part of the bounce. This grid also keeps the horse shorter and therefore carrying his weight more on his hindquarters, which improves his balance through the whole exercise. The work first shortens him and then lengthens him, improving his muscular elasticity.

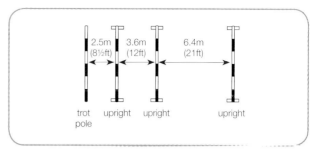

Canter grid

A development on a simple, straight grid is to increase the distances to enable you to approach in canter. In this grid, a placing pole is put 2.7m (9ft) away from a small parallel. There is a second small parallel 10m (33ft) from the first parallel and a third small parallel 11m (36ft) from this. Begin with a single parallel and add elements as your horse becomes more proficient.

You can set up the grid to have either one or two strides between fences. Parallels encourage the horse to open out and, if there is a short distance between fences, he has to close again. This lengthening and shortening through the exercise improves reactions and elasticity.

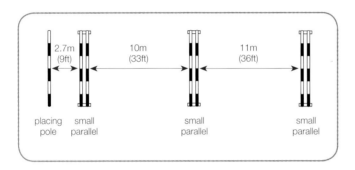

| placing pole | small parallel | 2.7m (9ft) | 10m (33ft) | small parallel | 11m (36ft) | small parallel |

Increasing athleticism

The basic canter grid can also be adjusted to help increase the horse's athleticism over each parallel and improve his ability to adjust his stride between fences. This is achieved by bringing forward the front rail of the parallels to make the spread wider. Initially, this is done with the second parallel and then with the third as well. The effect of this is to reduce the distances between the first and second parallel to 9m (30ft), and between the second and third parallel to 10m (33ft). By asking him to open himself up over the parallel and shorten on the ground, this grid works on the skills your horse has already gained, again increasing his elasticity and balance.

AIMS OF JUMP TRAINING

Whatever type of jump schooling you use, the objectives behind the training remain the same:

• To achieve calm approaches to fences, with both horse and rider confident in their abilities so that they can tackle whatever they meet – this is where learning to deal with all kinds of fences is vital (left and below left).

• To have the horse approaching in balance with an even length of stride, on a good line and in a consistent rhythm.

• For both horse and rider to have excellent balance during all phases of the jump (below).

• To produce good co-ordination in both horse and rider.

• To ensure the partnership is able to lengthen or shorten strides if required. The rider will need to know how many strides are necessary between fences and will have to make decisions in relation to this. For example, if your horse is better at shortening his stride, you may need to ask him to put in six strides rather than struggling to make five longer strides. However, you should also teach your horse how to lengthen his stride so that you can adjust it when necessary, as well as allowing him to think for himself.

• On the approach to this grid this horse is quite keen, which is good, but he will soon find that he needs to concentrate a little harder. The rider has to keep an even contact and allow the horse to learn for himself.

• The bounce distance between the two uprights causes him to shorten and creates active hindquarters – note the flexion of his hocks.

Engagement exercise

This grid is designed to improve the engagement of the hindquarters. It consists of a placing pole to an upright, then a bounce distance [approx 3.6m (12ft)] to another upright and then a stride [6.4–7.3m (21–24ft)] to a spread fence.

The placing pole to the first upright makes the horse start the exercise in the right balance, whether in trot or canter. The bounce makes the horse step under with the hind legs encouraging more engagement, while not becoming long because of the influence of the second element of the bounce. The short stride keeps the horse's weight back before the spread, which then opens the horse's back with the added effort needed to jump its width.

• He has succeeded. As he approaches and takes off, the horse's hindlegs are extremely active and well under him so providing lots of propulsive power.

• As the horse lands over the second upright fence, the controlled energy created by the bounce and the fact that he is not able to lengthen and flatten due to the second upright, results in maintainance of the activity, needed for the final fence.

   The rider needs to keep the horse going with this activity during the non-jumping stride in order to cope with the larger spread fence. He does this by having a consistent leg pressure into an even rein contact, without pulling back but without allowing the horse to run.

• As a result a good jump is produced over the spread fence. The rider needs to work on staying straighter in his position while looking forward instead of down. He is not, however, restricting his horse's ability to jump.

Grid to improve regularity of stride

The following exercise is useful for developing a regular stride pattern between two related fences and is used either for a horse that rushes and lengthens and flattens his stride between fences, or for a horse that shortens and hesitates (backing off), and therefore finds making jumps over a given distance difficult.

• In this grid to improve regularity of stride, two parallels are positioned with two non-jumping strides in between. There is a placing pole 2.7m (9ft) before the second element to control the length of stride prior to the point of take-off.

• With the same fences, a second pole is placed 3.3m (11ft) after the first parallel. This controls the length of the landing stride.

• Having jumped the exercise several times, the pair do it without the two ground poles to see if they can maintain the same balance and regularity throughout. All the rider must do is keep the horse in a balance and rhythm while remaining straight.

Grid to improve horse and rider responses

This grid consists of a bounce (that is, no non-jumping stride between two upright fences), then a stride, then another bounce between two upright fences. It is designed to test the reflexes of both you and your horse, as well as teach you to use your upper body to help control the pace. It is important that you do not become too quick in your position through this exercise, due to the sharp reactions of the horse in the first bounce. Keep your shoulders tall and slow and adopt a good line of sight as these will enable you to progress through the second bounce correctly.

• To ride a bounce well, the approach must be balanced, with plenty of controlled impulsion. If the approach is too fast, the horse will flatten and will not be able to pick up his feet in time. If the approach is too slow, he will lose his impulsion and will not be able to make the athletic effort necessary. The rider has to resist the temptation to tip forward due to the increased energy, but must be flexible enough to allow for the very quick action of the horse as he jumps the bounce.

• There is a non-jumping stride between the two sets of bounce fences, so the rider has to concentrate on keeping the activity generated by the first bounce, maintaining the rounded bouncy stride, but without going too fast, so that the pair can negotiate the second bounce. You can see that this time around the rider has lost his line of sight and allowed his right leg to swing back, something he will correct the next time he jumps through the exercise.

Jumping on an angle

A grid laid out as a straight line of fences can also be used for jumping at an angle. Using a grid in this way poses an extra question of control for the rider – if a horse is used to going straight down a line of fences, he may resist being asked to jump one fence in the grid at an angle. For example, he may stop or try to rush and take the whole grid on.

This grid consists of an upright to upright on one stride followed by a parallel on two strides. Before you attempt this exercise, jump some single fences on an angle first so that your horse is not taken by surprise.

Jumping grids like this helps the horse to concentrate on instructions from the rider, to listen and wait for aids rather than assuming he knows what to do. This attentiveness is vital for when you face more serious questions, such as when jumping accuracy fences on cross-country courses and when tackling fences on related distances.

• This horse obediently does as she is asked, jumping on an angle. Note how her off fore is left behind – this is because of the sequence of legs leaving the ground from canter. A split second later and her knees would be level.

VARY THE VENUE

It is fine to work your horse at home, but you should also try to have training sessions at many other venues so he learns to take new sights and sounds in his stride while still doing his work.

• She comes around again and this time jumps the second fence in the grid from a different angle. Jumping on an angle creates a challenge for the rider in that if you allow the horse to drift one way or the other, you lengthen or shorten the distance to the fence, or offer the horse the opportunity to run out.

• The pair then comes around once more and jumps the parallel in the same way, on an angle. This time the mare makes an extra effort and has much sharper action in her forelegs.

• Having completed several rounds of jumping on the angle, the mare is asked to jump straight through. Note how her foreleg technique is good from the beginning of the grid. Jumping on angles can sharpen a horse's reactions. For example, a horse that is not very sharp in front will not necessarily benefit from going straight down a grid, but jumping on an angle means she must become sharper in her technique.

Jumping on circles and curves

Jumping on a circle is not as easy as it sounds. First practise with four evenly spaced poles on the ground on a 20-m (65-ft) circle. Start off in trot, ensuring you maintain the rhythm and balance as you describe a circle and pop over each pole. If your flatwork is lacking, you'll probably find it hard to keep your horse on the correct line; he may well fall in or out, and you may be adding to the problems by over-correcting him with your rein aids. Remove the poles and place a small fence on the circle. Staying in trot, pop over the fence, keeping the same discipline over the circle line. Remember to ride the circle on both reins as both you and your horse will have a favourite side.

Once you have mastered it in trot, try the exercise in canter. Establish your rhythm before coming on to the circle, and try to maintain the same rhythm and the correct circle line. If your horse lands on the wrong leg, trot and pick up the correct leg again. Try to encourage the horse to land on the correct leg by keeping your outside leg on so that he does not push out as he takes off over the fences. This type of controlled work is very tiring, so give your horse plenty of chances to stretch and recover.

• Plan your route carefully – look around your circle towards your fence in plenty of time.

• Approach in trot – master this before you try to carry out the exercise in canter. The trot must be active but balanced and not running. Keep a little bend within the inside contact but support the outside of the horse with the outside contact and outside leg. Your inside leg keeps the horse out into the outside aids.

• Work equally on both reins doing four or five circles before changing the rein. All horses are one-sided and will find the exercise easier in one direction. This horse is making a better effort on this rein, which might be because he is stronger off one hind leg than the other. This shows that this exercise has a good muscular development potential.

• Allow your horse to use his head and neck as he negotiates the fence, but maintain a contact so that you can guide him around the circle. Ride the jumping circle exactly as you would a circle on the flat, using the same aids, but take into account the fact that the horse will drift more easily in the air (ie over the fence) so use your outside aids to support the circle line more at this point. Use your line of sight to look around the circle to aid direction.

• Once you are proficient at jumping on a circle, practise changing the rein over the fence. Here, the rider has come in off the left rein, negotiated the fence and is already thinking of turning right as she jumps the fence. In order to change the rein, change your line of sight, indicate the new direction with the new inside rein and push the horse onto the new line with the new outside aids.

A grid across the B–E line

This grid has two fences – a spread and an upright – placed across the B–E line with one non-jumping stride in between them. The distance from the fence to the first jump is 7.3m (24ft). The exercise demands control, balance and impulsion from the turn on to the B–E line – this turn is crucial because if you get it wrong the ensuing jump will be poor. The exercise should be ridden off either rein – one way will be much easier for your horse.

• You can see here that the turn on to the line is not easy – this horse seems to be 'motorbiking' around it. The rider has allowed the mare to fall in around the turn so she is very much on her inside shoulder. She needs to ride the horse much more upright from the inside leg to the outside aids. In the second photograph, it is clear from the horse's hindquarters that, as a result of a poorly prepared and executed turn, she has lost balance and impulsion. However, her genuine character and jumping ability shows as the pair still manage to negotiate the first fence neatly and efficiently. Their experience comes to the fore as they get themselves together and arrive at the second fence in a much more balanced manner.

• With a bit of practice, the horse realizes that rushing is not to her advantage and the rider leaves less to chance and works on keeping the horse upright by working her from the inside aids to the outside aids. As a result, they make a better approach with improved balance around the turn.

• Having completed the exercise on the left rein, the combination rides it on the right rein. It is clear that this is the rider's preferred rein as the balance is so much better through the turn and over the first fence.

The 'either way' grid

In this development of the grid that runs across the B–E line, the rider negotiates a fence on the B–E line and then turns either right or left to another fence at right angles to the first.

Set up the grid with a placing pole to a fence situated on the B–E line – put the jump 7.3m (24ft) from the track with the placing pole 2.5m (8½ft) before it – then position one fence at right angles to the left of the B–E line (here three strides distance, or 13.7–14.4m/45–48ft) and another at right angles to the right of the B–E line (here four strides distance, or 17.3–18.3m/57–60ft).

Riders must keep the approach balanced and controlled in order to negotiate the first fence. They also have to keep their line of sight horizontal to the ground so that they can ride the correct line to whichever of the two right-angled fence, they plan to negotiate. On landing over the first fence, they must quickly re-establish their upright position and balance the horse, ready for the curving turn to the next fence.

This exercise works on developing balance on more advanced turns and on your horse's responsiveness to changes of direction. It is particularly beneficial when practising for jump-offs.

• The rider approaches from the left turn and makes a departure to the right to the parallel (a distance of four strides away).

• Having made a good turn to the right, the pair jump the fence well.

• Here the approach is from the right turn with a departure to the left on three strides to the upright.

• This turn is not made so smoothly. The horse is leaning a little left and needs to be more upright, which could be achieved by the rider using stronger aids from the inside to the outside.

Building your skills

Ensure your jump training follows a logical order. Introduce the horse to various designs of fence individually before tackling several types together. Start off with simple trotting poles, cross poles, simple uprights and narrow spreads. John prefers not to use cross poles with inexperienced horses as he feels punishing a youngster for not being straight at an early part of its training can be detrimental. Instead, he uses a simple low upright which puts the onus on the rider to produce straightness. Once a young horse is jumping confidently, cross poles can be very effective.

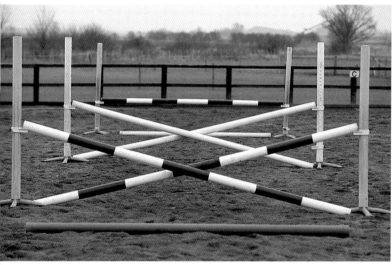

• **Cross rails** Cross rails, where two poles cross in the middle between two wings, may be used on their own as a training fence or as part of a fence. For example, they might make up the first element of a spread. When used on their own, in training, the shape is intended to encourage the horse towards the centre of the fence.

• **Ascending verticals** This is a simple upright with a pole placed in front of the fence at a distance of about half the height of the fence. This ground line helps the horse gauge his take-off so that he does not get too close to the fence and hit it. Ascending verticals are particularly useful for warming up horses that can be a bit lazy in front. Once the horse is jumping correctly, the ground pole can be moved closer.

• **Ascending spreads** A triple bar is an example of an ascending spread and one that often worries riders. Anxiety about making the width of the fence often causes over-riding to it, resulting in a bad jump. Such fences need to be ridden with an active, forward round canter so that the horse can be deep to the front rail and gain both height and width.

• **Training spread** With a training spread the low front rail allows the horse to be deep to the base of the fence and the double back rail makes him really release his back to jump. John Bowen uses this fence to relax the horse's back and increase overall suppleness when a horse is tight. He finds it particularly useful during warm-up for competitions.

Types of fences

Always consider your horse in the design of your fences and the questions you ask. When you build fences, ensure they are on a good footing and fairly sturdy. Flimsy fences are dangerous and can make a horse lose confidence. Use good solid poles, too, as they will help a horse learn from his mistakes, which he won't do if the poles are too light. Never try to trick a horse with groundlines behind fences or use any techniques that might make him question his judgement – a loss of confidence or trust can be irreparable.

• **True vertical** Once your horse is jumping ascending verticals correctly, it is time to introduce a true vertical as the next step in his development and education. This example shows a true vertical using two poles.

• **Walls, gates and planks** are also examples of true verticals – there is no ground line, just a series of poles on the wings. The ideal take-off point is the same distance away as the height of the fence.

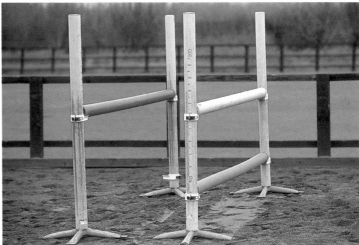

• **Oxers** Oxers may be true or ascending, but they are always a spread. In a true oxer the front and back rails are at the same height – to the horse (and the rider) the fence can look like a vertical. The highest point of the horse's jump should be over the centre of the spread; the ideal take-off point is one-and-a-half times the height of the fence away from this central point. An ascending oxer differs from an ascending spread in that the poles are always parallel to each other, whereas in an ascending spread the fence might be wider on one side than the other.

Varying your approach

Once your horse is jumping confidently, you can vary your lines of approach. The sequence below shows an angled approach, which this horse and rider have ridden in a good balance on a good line – with excellent results.

Jumping on turns

Turns from one fence to another can be more of a challenge than you might think. You need to control the amount of bend and concentrate on maintaining the horse's balance and alignment through the turn.

• During a turn from a yellow and red fence (above left) to a green and yellow parallel (left and above) this horse has grabbed the bit and the rider was caught out. If a problem occurs during a turn, reassess your pace, balance and control.

• When the pair repeat the exercise making corrections – keeping an even contact and equal leg aids – they clear the jump beautifully.

• You can see that the horse is already drifting through the right shoulder as the pair jump the first fence.

Coping with common problems
Balance and pace on a straight line

Maintaining correct balance and pace on a straight line can be a challenge. Here you can see that the horse is becoming a little quick down a straight line of three fences and is also drifting through his right shoulder. This rider would benefit from doing a couple of circles to settle the canter before she starts. Then she should think slow and make sure she is not too quick with her shoulders. Using the voice can also settle a horse through an exercise.

• As they land, the rider has achieved some more straightness, but you can see that the horse is a little quick and intense.

• A drift that continues on landing…

• With the result that he starts to drift again over the second fence.

• … and on the approach to the final fence the horse continues to drift and now the rider is starting to become crooked through tension as well.

Balance and direction on turns

Maintaining balance and direction on turns between fences is another area that has its pitfalls. This rider has insufficient control over balance, pace and direction on a right turn, which has resulted in a run out to the left. She would benefit from schoolwork that includes circles and turns to improve her control of bend. She needs to learn to use more strength in the outside aids and slightly less on the inside ones.

• As the pair round the corner the rider has asked for too much right bend and the horse is running through the left shoulder. Although she tries to straighten the horse's neck to approach the fence, the loss of control has already happened.

• The horse continues on his sideways travel and the loss of control escalates...

• ...leading to a run out to the left.

Lack of control

If there is a lack of control or influence over balance, line and pace, it is more difficult to jump fences rhythmically, which is necessary if you are to complete a round of fences in good time without faults. As a result of poor control, a horse will often run a little deep to the fence, stand off too far, or even run out or stop through a lack of confidence.

• The rider has used too much left rein on the approach to the fence, but has no control of the horse's right side, with the result that he runs out.

• The pair repeats the exercise and the horse becomes more relaxed, beginning to maintain the line easily. Initially, the resulting jump may not feel comfortable but with repetition the horse will become more confident.

• Work on pace, balance and line pays off. The horse's neck is straighter – showing that the rider's aids are more balanced – and although still a little tense, he becomes more relaxed with each repetition.

• This young horse has run a little too close to the fence and, due to excess speed and tension caused by inexperience, is on his forehand and out of balance (top left). As he tries to extricate himself from this situation, his jump loses fluidity and balance, resulting in the rider getting in front of the movement (above). The highest point of the jump is well beyond the fence (left), instead of over the fence. This means that the hindlegs trail and the horse knocks the fence over.

• Later in the same training session you can see the improvement in the same horse's technique after emphasis has been placed upon improving his balance and rhythm when jumping by riding transitions, turns and circles and using the voice to settle him through these exercises, both on the flat and over fences.

Putting fences together

Practising turns and jumping one or two fences is fine, but you need to put everything together to compete successfully. The objective of setting up a realistic jumping course at home is to practise riding in the correct balance, in the correct pace, riding turns and distances you might meet in competition. In a school arena you can ride the same line or turn several times so that you no longer find them difficult. By identifying areas of weakness and working on them in the peace of familiar surroundings you can start to overcome them and then transfer the improvements into the competition environment. Work done at home will pay dividends in the competition ring. Once you feel you have sufficient control over pace, balance and correctness, add a few fences together, making sure there are some turns and straight lines, and use these to work towards jumping a course. If any problems occur, iron them out as you go by repeating the exercise a few times or go back to a grid, an earlier exercise or a smaller jump. Any loss of control or alignment will spoil the quality of the jump.

Turns

There are three key elements to turns: the sharper the turn, the more you are likely to have problems; several turns in the same direction are easier to make than several in different directions; the number of strides around a turn will have an influence on how easy the turn will be. Bear these in mind when walking a course.

• Off a right turn this rider pushes her horse forward too much by using her seat. The horse has gone onto his forehand and his head is too high.

• As he comes over the jump, he cramps his back. There is also visible tightness in the rider, who has a poor leg position.

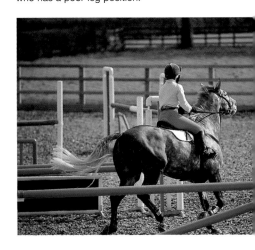

• You can see here how low the horse is in his shoulders, which will make it difficult for him to jump.

• He has tried to drop his neck and lift his shoulders but he is tense through his topline, resulting in a poor jump.

• The horse lands very much on the forehand.

• The combination then continue the turn in a tense out-of-balance canter.

• This tension and lack of balance make the approach to the next fence quite uncomfortable. Had the rider used more leg and less seat through the first turn, the horse would have remained much rounder through his length and therefore much softer through this sequence.

• This horse and rider jump into the exercise with a very correct jump – everything is in balance.

• They make a good departure with the rider already thinking about the turn.

• Through the turn the rider controls the horse's neck; even though he is a little high with his neck, his back stays round because the rider's seat is not 'down in the saddle'.

• Note that the horse has an 'uphill' balance. This helps him to maintain impulsion and make the next jump.

• The pair tackle the fence in style, with the rider holding her line of sight. Although she has remained out of the saddle, she is not in front of the movement.

• They produce a very correct jump with an equally good technique.

• The rider controls the horse on the outside on this turn.

• The mare starts to run to the fence, but the rider supports her well with both legs and both reins.

• By the time they reach the fence, the mare has drifted left and changed lead. Had the rider not been in control, they would have had a run out, especially as their route takes them to the left after the fence.

• The balanced control of the rider has created the opportunity for the horse to make her jump.

• And the result is a very good jump, from a tricky ride around the turn.

Different lines

When riding lines in practice or in a competition, it is important that you know which ones may cause more difficulty. Remember that to reach each fence correctly, you must be able to ride exactly on the line you have walked (see p.77). Make sure you are able to jump some of the individual lines well before tackling the whole course.

• This horse and rider have approached a line of two fences from a right-hand turn.

• The horse was not sufficiently under control on his outside (left) and has drifted through the left shoulder as he jumps the first fence.

• The pair continue to drift to the next fence...

• When they attempt the pair of fences a second time, the rider has corrected her mistake. She has much more control of the horse's left side.

• They remain straight over the jumps and the rider retains good control over the left side.

Two jumps on a straight line

Although it might seem reasonably straightforward to jump two fences that are on a straight line, it is still necessary to work on encouraging straightness and balance when jumping from one fence to another. The sequences below reveal why it is important and show improving straightness through the same pair of fences.

• ...jumping it well over to the left. Whether the next fence is straight ahead, or on a turn to the left or to the right, it is clear that the approach will be affected by this lack of straightness.

• They clear the second fence still on the correct line, although you can still see the 'thought' of going left.

Turns

The way you negotiate a turn dictates the balance with which you arrive at the fence, and therefore your chances of clearing it neatly and correctly. It is very important to develop and improve balance and uprightness around a turn without allowing the horse to fall in onto his inside shoulder (top row, centre) or drift out and lose his outside shoulder. Be aware that if only half of the horse's energy is correctly aligned there is only 50 percent of the power to jump the fence correctly (middle row, centre).

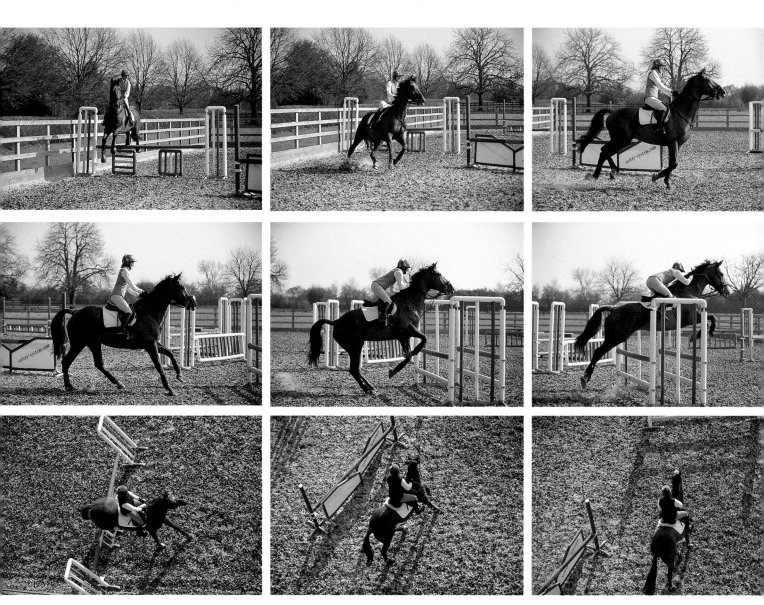

• This exercise of two fences on a turn reveals very clearly the importance of control and the ability to ride the exact line that you walked. If you cut the corner, you will reach the second fence half a stride too short, and if you allow your horse to drift out, you will be half a stride too long. A horse that tightens around corners will be 'tight' at the point of take-off, making it more difficult to jump correctly.

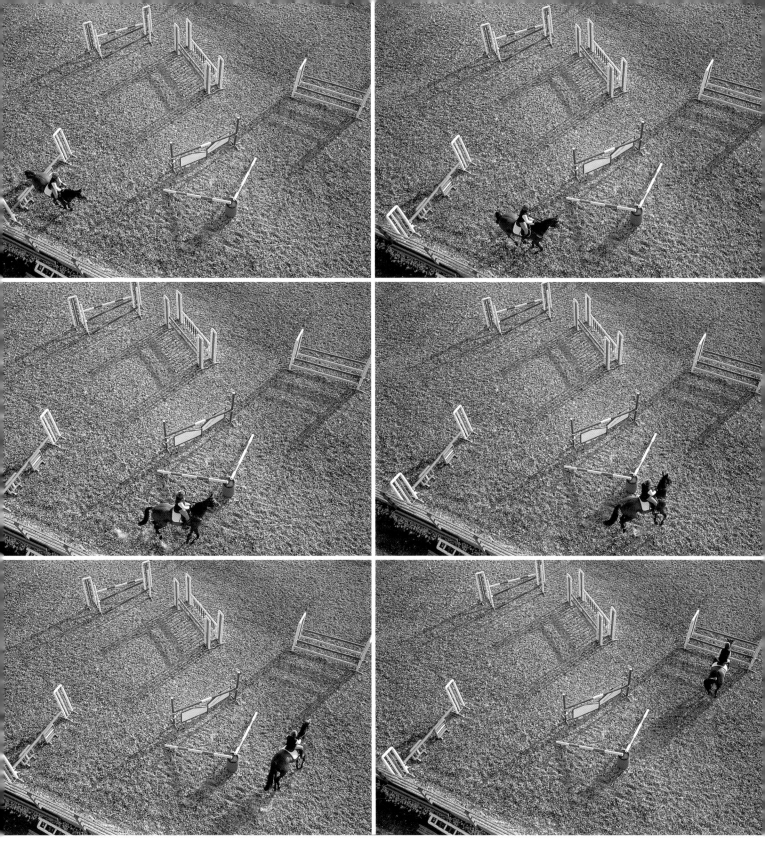

• To counteract tightening around a corner, place a barrel and two poles on the turn to help make it more balanced and achieve a more accurate presentation to the second fence. Using the barrel and poles encourages the rider to push the horse around the barrel with the inside leg, while still controlling the outside. In the sequence above, you can see how upright the horse has become – he is no longer leaning to the left. The rider is also upright, and very central in the middle of the horse. Practise these corrections over the same set of fences in both directions.

Test Your Progress
An angled approach

When you have practised jumping different lines and turns, test your horse's responses and see what sort of progress you are both making by jumping the middle fence within a line of three with an angled approach. Being able to choose a fence and jump it from any angle is a good test of how well your horse concentrates on what you are asking of him. This test will soon reveal whether or not he is distracted by the other jumps and whether or not he is on your aids.

A dog leg

Jumping a dog leg from one fence to another
is another good exercise to check your control over
balance, rhythm and line. This pair excute the test
well.

This course has been designed to include most of the problems you would meet in a competition, except a true combination. Some of the fences are jumped twice, and it can be ridden in reverse order – this maximizes resources. Or ride the course in reverse order. This way the difficult turns are at the start of the course.

- The easiest route around this course is shown by the white lines and starts on the left rein to a blue upright (1).

- Then there is a soft curved line on four strides to a green upright (2), continuing on a soft left curved line to a blue and white upright (3).

- There is a left-hand line around the white and yellow stile (7), then an approach to a multi-coloured parallel (4) with a departure line to the right, jumping a double from blue upright (5) to yellow and green parallel (6) on two strides.

- The course continues on a straight line on three strides to the yellow and while stile (7), continuing the turn to the right around fence three, jumping the blue and yellow upright (8).

- There follows a dog leg to another double – red and white upright (9), two strides to a red and white parallel (10).

- A left turn after the parallel leads to fence two (green and yellow upright) to be jumped again followed by a right-angled turn left to the red and yellow parallel (12) with a departure line straight on and around the yellow and white stile (7).

- Finally there is a right-handed approach to jump fence three in the opposite direction.

- When you are proficient at the first course practise tighter jump-off lines by following the 12-fence course marked by the dashed yellow line.

Using the course

This sequence shows a young horse negotiating the course (see pp.70–71). The object of this course is to test the ability of the horse and rider to maintain balance and rhythm on the kind of different lines that they will meet in competition. At this height, 1m (3ft), the course can be jumped several times, giving the horse a short break between rounds, to work on any individual problems that may need addressing during the training session.

• Here, the horse, having jumped fences 1 and 2, continues on a correct line to the centre of fence 3. If the rider had not maintained the correct balance between fences 2 and 3, the horse could have drifted through his right shoulder and jumped fence 3 up against the right wing or even run past the fence. Thanks to their correct training and discipline, the horse and rider are in the correct balance and on the correct line for the third fence. Their departure line from this fence takes them around the yellow and white upright – the rider should be thinking about maintaining the same balance and rhythm around this upright.

• The combination jumps fence 4, which involves making a change of direction and therefore the balance and line is doubly important. At this stage, the rider must not allow the horse to anticipate changing the rein and therefore end up drifting to the right over the multi-coloured parallel. She must be disciplined enough to land and take the first non-jumping stride before even thinking about the turn.

• As they continue around the course, the horse and rider remain in the correct balance. They are seen here jumping the centre of the yellow upright, which is the third fence in a line of three. The rider could so easily have drifted left or right by this stage on a long line of fences if she had not been disciplined about her line of sight (which needs to be forwards and into the distance – see p.11). Obviously the balance and rhythm was maintained well enough around the entire course, for a horse at this level of training, as none of the fences have been knocked down.

Coping with problems

Riding this course is a good test of how your training is progressing. Any weaknesses in your control of rhythm, pace and balance on straight lines and turns will be shown up, enabling you to work on them using the exercises outlined throughout this section. Make use of simple repetition over elements of this course to work on individual problem areas.

• This young horse (right) is a little long in his frame and too forward in his canter so he has reached the fence 'on a long one' and consequently is jumping flat and across the fence rather than up and over it.

• This rider has reached a good point of take off in a correct balance and the horse is using himself correctly over this parallel. The good jump is achieved partly due to the rider achieving an active, balanced and controlled canter on the approach.

JUMPING THE COURSE IN REVERSE

This course is designed to be jumped in both directions, which makes it more versatile for training purposes. Make sure that all jumps are jumpable from both directions, with poles and fillers correct on both sides. Jumped in reverse, this course poses more difficult questions at the beginning with the tricky turns coming early, then finishes with the easy lines.

SEEING A STRIDE

It's very easy to become over-analytical about seeing a stride and reaching a correct point of take off for a fence. However, the good news is that you can only ever be half-a-stride wrong at a fence; if a horse is in the correct balance, has impulsion and is in front of the rider's leg, he will usually jump far more easily when half-a-stride out than if he reaches the correct point of take-off in the wrong balance and without impulsion.

• The horse has been allowed to run in a little deep and on his forehand and is therefore unable to come up in his shoulders correctly. Working on the quality of the canter, enabling it to become shorter and more on the hindlegs, will improve this horse's ability to 'wait'.

• The same horse arriving at a better take-off point in a much improved balance, achieved through work to make his canter more active. The horse can now 'wait', with his weight towards his hindquarters, which enables him to lift his shoulders and jump much more athletically.

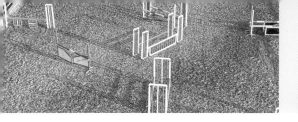

Jumping in competition

During a show-jumping round a horse will be tested on his ability to jump different types of obstacles, some of which will be on related distances, perhaps with a more difficult approach, such as on a dog leg instead of a straight line.

Show courses usually consist of around 12 jumps and may include combinations such as a double or a treble. Water jumps, either in the form of water trays, or open water with small brushes in front, may also be used. The course builder will aim to enable a certain percentage of the entrants achieve a clear round without causing too much grief for the less able horses or riders. He can use a mix of fences – spreads, planks, gates, water, combination and so on – but it is the way that he arranges the collection of fences that tests the riders. For instance, a horse needs to meet a triple bar on a forward-going stride to make the spread easily. However, if the course builder sets up a gate as the next fence, just four or five strides away, then the rider has to be quick to balance the horse after the spread of the triple bar and regain a shorter, bouncier stride from which to tackle this

upright fence. This is where experience counts. For example, an inexperienced rider could collapse forward after the triple bar and then need a couple of strides to regain balance and control, which means she might find it difficult to clear the upright.

The course builder can also test riders by placing fences on dog legs rather than straight lines as the control required is greater. Placing fences off turns also makes things more challenging, as does siting fences so that the horse has to turn away from the ring exit. One of the reasons for walking the course is to note how the course has been designed in this respect and decide whether it will help or hinder your horse.

KNOW THE RULES

Once you start to compete, it is vital that you know the rules – schedules will often state that a class is run under Rules ABC, etc, so you do have to be familiar with the rules in order to know what to do. Rules can also change so do not rely on the knowledge you had when you last competed 10 years ago!

• When walking the course, note which type of jump follows on from each fence. If, for instance, a triple bar like this is followed by an upright just a few strides away, it will be more demanding of horse and rider than if it were the last fence on the course.

WALKING THE COURSE

One of the most important preparations when jumping is knowing the layout and distances of the course or your exercises. Setting up small courses at home and practising course-walking will improve your ability to ride correct lines, whether these are straight, curves or turns.

• A rider walking a straight line between a parallel and an upright.

• A rider walking a right turn from one parallel to another parallel.

For distances between fences the rule of thumb is:
• allow two human strides from the fence for the horse's landing;
• allow four human strides for one non-jumping stride of the horse;
• allow two human strides for take-off.

This means that:

• if there are eight human strides between fences there is enough room for one horse stride between the fences;

• if there are 11 or 12 human strides, there is room for two horse strides;

• if there are 15 or 16 human strides, there is room for three horse strides and so on.

Jump-off technique

Success in a jump-off is not about speed but economy of line. Watch a top show jumper such as John Whitaker and you'll see him taking strides out in between fences and around turns so that his time is extremely competitive and his horse has the best chance of jumping fences cleanly. This is achieved by planning the route, looking ahead and maintaining the horse's balance and rhythm throughout. It is not achieved by simply going fast – speed results in the horse losing balance and rhythm and jumping flatly so he knocks fences down.

Jumping on a circle

These two exercises are aimed at helping you and your horse make tighter approaches, which will improve your jump-off times. At this stage, keep the jumps quite small (those shown here are 76–84cm (2ft 6in–2ft 9in). Both exercises help the partnership in maintaining balance, rhythm and line; adding more fences on the circle makes this progressively more difficult. You need to concentrate on your balanced position – any time you have spent practising the jumping position on circles and turns on the flat will pay off now. Start off with a 20-m (65-ft) circle and progress to using more jumps or making the circle smaller. (If you experience difficulties, go back a stage, see p.44.)

Before you start practising jump off techniques you need to be jumping clear around the first rounds, maintaining a good balance and rhythm and riding the exact line that you walked.

• **Jumping one fence on a circle** This is an introductory exercise to improving jump-off technique for both horse and rider. It is also invaluable for basic schooling over fences as varying the line of approach is beneficial to a young horse's education: once she has learned to jump two fences on a straight line, you can introduce jumping on a circle, which will teach her not to rush. As you ride the circle, think about keeping the rhythm of the pace so that the horse is jumping out of her stride; you also need to concentrate hard on keeping the shape of the circle. Do this exercise on both reins, but always start on the rein she finds easier.

• **Jumping two to four fences on a circle** As a development of the first exercise, add another fence. With a young horse, add the second fence on the circle at a point opposite the first one so that there is half a circle between each fence. For a more advanced horse, you could put the second fence at the next quarter point on the circle. Eventually a more advanced horse (intermediate level) will learn to jump four fences on a circle, a fence being placed at each quarter point. Concentrate on the rhythm and balance as before. Vary the line of approach on the circle so that if you jump on an inside line, you'll be jumping on four strides, if you approach on the outside line you'll be jumping on five strides.

EXERCISES FOR MAKING QUICKER TURNS

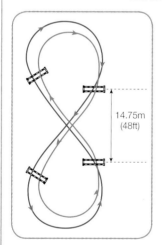

Simple figure of eight

Riding this grid (left) will help you practise economic turns so you reduce the number of strides it takes to complete the exercise. Ride at a normal speed and count the number of strides. Then ride a shorter line, making tighter turns, counting the strides to discover how many you can save. Work on both reins as one will be easier than the other.

14.75m
(48ft)

Advanced figure of eight

The diagram (right) shows a more advanced figure of eight exercise combining two 20-m (65-ft) circles and seven jumps. The small parallel fence is in the centre while the remaining fences are all small uprights. Start off with three fences (marked A) in a line – ie parallel and upright either side, which can be jumped on a circle on both reins. Then circle, change over the parallel onto a new circle in the opposite direction, continue round this circle and then change over the parallel back onto your original circle. You can then jump up and down the three fences on a continual figure of eight. Now build up to the ultimate exercise by adding two more upright fences (marked B) to each circle. Maintain the discipline of riding the circles correctly and do not cut any corners. If the fences are set out correctly you will get the same number of strides between each fence each time – usually four non-jumping strides. To make it really advanced and applicable to jump-off techniques, practise riding an outside line, so adding an extra stride, eg five strides between each fence. Then practise an inside line, taking away a stride, ie three strides between each fence.

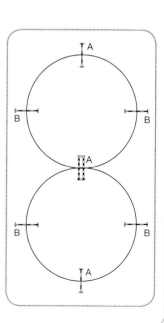

• **Jumping on the angle** In a jump-off course it might save seconds and give you a better line to another fence if you can jump a preceding fence on an angle. Once a horse is used to jumping and has learnt to go exactly where her rider says, jumping on an angle is not a problem. The only point you have to watch is if you jump a spread, as the angle may increase the spread too much.

• **Making quicker turns** This is where attention to schooling on the flat will have paid dividends. The secret to a successful turn is to keep the horse balanced and the engine running, that is to have his hindquarters sufficiently engaged underneath him so that he can turn quickly and move on, without slipping or running wide. Be careful that you do not overdo the use of the inside rein as you turn and beware of tipping your own body in your enthusiasm to make the turn.

Cross-country jumping

Riding across country, jumping solid fences, requires confidence in both horse and rider, and they must have trust in each other. To enjoy the job, both halves of the partnership must have been well prepared so that they know they can tackle anything on the competition course. Although the competition is where horse and rider test their skill and courage, the important work is done at home, during the education of the pair. There can be no short cuts in cross-country training – to overlook any skills or steps is reckless. For you and your horse to progress safely, you need to put in the groundwork and get the mileage and experience under your belts before you move up a level.

You can practise certain elements of cross-country jumping in the arena. When you are ready to go out on to a practice course, ask your instructor and an experienced horse and rider combination to accompany you. Inexperienced or young horses will be given confidence by the presence of another horse and can take advantage of the lead he can offer.

EQUIPMENT FOR HORSE AND RIDER

Rider

- **Skull cap** Well fitting, latest standard skull cap and silk.

- **Body protector** Choose a good quality, safety-tested and approved protector with shoulder pads as extra protection. If you buy a protector from a reputable retailer, they should be trained in fitting. Take advantage of this service to ensure you have the best possible protection.

- **Stock** This can be kept firmly in place with the use of safety pins.

- **Whip** It is advisable to carry a whip as you may need it. A rubber-gripped top makes a whip easier to hold. Some people put a martingale rein stop at the top of the whip to help prevent it slipping through their hands.

- **Spurs** You never know when you might need the extra attention and response a spur can provide. Ensure any whips or spurs do not exceed the dimensions laid down in the rule book.

- **Gloves** These are very useful for extra grip. The type and style is a matter of personal preference, but remember that leather gloves can become slippery when wet with water or sweat.

- **Breeches, riding boots and cross-country colours** Make sure your riding clothes fit well and are comfortable.

Horse

- **Bridle** If you fall off over your horse's head, it is possible to take the bridle with you. To prevent this, tie a bootlace around the headpiece and secure the bridle to the top plait on the horse's neck.

- **Bit** Control is essential so select the bit that best suits your horse. Remember that horses may show pain or discomfort in their mouths by tossing their head around, by being difficult to turn or stop, by leaning on the bit, and so on. Take your horse's mouth conformation into account when selecting a bit – make sure he has enough room in his mouth.

- **Breastplate** This will help prevent the saddle from slipping backwards as you jump up and down steps and drops. A neckstrap can provide additional security, should you need it.

- **Martingale** If one is required.

- **Jumping saddle** Choose one according to your preference, but make sure it fits the horse well. Have the fit checked regularly. Check the stitching on the saddle, girth and stirrup leathers. Use a surcingle or overgirth as extra security.

- **Boots** Select the type according to your horse's needs and your preference. If they have velcro fastenings, tape over them for added security. If you use bandages, they should be stitched as well, in order to keep them in place.

- **Studs** These may be used for extra security of footing. A variety will be needed to cope with all weather conditions – large square ones for heavy ground or soft mud, small pointed ones for slippery going, such as that caused by a rain shower on firm going. Whether you use studs on one or both branches of a shoe is a matter of personal preference as there are arguments for and against both.

- Before setting out on a schooling or competitive round it's vital to make a thorough check of all of your tack. It may sound obvious, but cross-country jumping is demanding enough without adding the risk of worn or damaged equipment letting you down. Replace your hat if there's a possibility it may have taken any impact in a fall.

Cantering

When the combination tackle the same slope in canter, it is clear how the balance of both horse and rider has to change as they negotiate a rise, a dip in the ground and then continue up a steeper slope. Note that although the rider's position changes, her balance in the saddle and her line of sight remain correct throughout the changes in the terrain. This is vital for safe cross-country riding, especially as you add more speed as your training progresses.

The rider has slightly leaned forward but maintains an uphill balance as the horse canters up the slope. An uphill balance is achieved by the rider being 'tall' with her shoulders and looking forward, not down, which would be more inclined to make her fall forward and rest on the horse's neck.

As the ground levels out, the rider becomes more upright in her position to maintain her balance in the centre of the horse and over the centre of gravity.

She maintains this position as the horse canters into the dip so that she stays in balance with the horse.

As they come out of the dip and the ground rises to a steeper slope, the rider inclines a little more forward, again staying with the horse's centre of gravity, which moves forward as he begins to negotiate the slope.

The horse has to use himself more effectively to be able to continue at speed and within the same balance.

BETWEEN FENCES

Practising cantering on different terrain makes it much easier to maintain your balance when cantering between fences on a cross-country course. This rider is making the most of the opportunities offered on a cross-country schooling day.

When the horse and rider canter down the same slope, the principles are the same as cantering through the small dip, but the engagement of the horse's hindlegs has to be increased in order for him to maintain his balance on a steeper slope. Note how his balance changes underneath the rider as he canters downhill. He takes more weight onto the hindlegs, which stops him running on his shoulders. The rider's line of sight enables her to maintain her balance. She comes out of the saddle so that she doesn't land on the horse's back with each stride. It is important to keep riding forwards downhill so that the horse doesn't prop – put his weight onto the forehand and shorten his stride in a backwards fashion.

CANTERING DOWNHILL

Narrow fences on lines and curves

Once you are jumping individual narrow fences confidently, the next step is to string several skinny fences together on straight lines and curves. Using the guide poles at first will encourage straightness throughout the exercise. The object of this exercise is to encourage the horse to remain upright on a disciplined line, without drifting left or right between the fences. Remember that it is the rider's leg, seat and upper body position that control the line and the balance, and the rider's elastic contact that guides the horse.

• In this sequence horse and rider jump two half barrels with guide poles on a soft curve to the right, to an arrowhead with guide poles leading up to it. A curving line follows this second fence to the left jumping a single filler between two jump stands with guide poles.

This horse and rider combination have become a little quick from fence two to three but the line is maintained satisfactorily for this level of training. Repetition will settle the horse and allow the exercise to be ridden in a more fluent manner. This is not a pull-push-pull exercise and should be ridden with softness and feel through the reins.

Introducing cross-country schooling

The purpose of the cross-country practice sessions is to build your horse's trust and confidence and extend his education so that he is capable of dealing with the questions he will be asked in competition. In your early schooling sessions, keep the fences small, so that if your horse makes a mistake he is not punished unduly – by a nasty fall, for instance. All the demands should be within your capabilities and those of your horse; as his confidence and experience grows, so more complex questions can be asked. In all schooling sessions, take note of how your horse is coping and stop before he becomes tired – mistakes are likely to be made when a horse becomes mentally or physically tired. It's better to end your session early on a good note than push things too far, create a problem for yourself and have an unsatisfactory ending.

The first few times you go cross-country schooling, aim to repeat the same fences and questions you have asked previously, and then build on this by adding one or two new questions each time. It's important that the horse finds these initial schooling sessions easy and does not associate his early cross-country sessions with bad experiences. Confidence is the foundation of correct cross-country riding.

FINDING A CLINIC

You can go cross-country schooling by hiring a course and taking an experienced friend or a trainer with you or by joining in one of the many clinics that are run around the country by various trainers. Clinics may be held over more than one day, and some trainers prefer to work through exercises in the arena, prior to going out on the cross-country course.

Cross-country clinic 1

Clinic 1 was taken by John at Somerford Park in Cheshire. The clinic involved a variety of horses ranging from Introduction level to Novice, and participants jumped a selection of fences, including simple tyres, steps, ditches, sunken road, coffins and different water fences. In this type of clinic John works on developing correct balance, rhythm and jumping technique in the horse and correct position and line of sight in the rider. He also aims to ensure that rider and horse work in harmony.

Remember to start each new training session by going over familiar ground as a refresher and to build confidence so that you do not overface yourself or your horse.

Warming up

During warm-up, aim to achieve the following:

• a balance and rhythm that can be maintained.

• a truly active horse.

• a horse that is in front of your leg.

• a horse that is carrying you forward positively, confidently and fluently with you in a good balance on his back.

• When warming up, try to be constructive by making changes of pace within the canter and changes of direction, including turns and circles, to make your horse supple and obedient for the questions ahead.

• The warm-up is an ideal time to check the length of your stirrups so that you can ride in a correct balance with a light seat, allowing the horse to work underneath you. This rider is showing good balance – her heels are below her seat, her knee is relaxed, she has a light jumping seat and her shoulders are not too far forward over the horse's centre of balance. Her line of sight is forward and parallel to the ground.

As you work through the schooling exercises that follow, remember these essentials and work to maintain all of them.

Find a straightforward simple fence that you can jump in both directions from straight lines and circles or turns. Use this first fence constructively, ensuring that your horse is balanced and obedient in both directions. It is fair to expect the horse to take several minutes to settle in the initial stages, and repetition of the exercise will relax him enough to be able proceed with the schooling session. Jumping a simple fence several times also enables you to think about your balance and position on approach, over the fence and on departure from the fence.

• This horse is jumping freely over the tyres and the rider is in good balance. The rider is maintaining a good line of sight, parallel to the ground.

• Instead of being parallel to it, this rider's line of sight is down to the ground. As a result, her upper body is in front of the movement and she falling forward, which in turn rotates her lower leg backwards, so weakening her position.

• This sequence shows it is not as easy as it looks. Although they cleared the tyres well the first time (top left), this horse and rider combination has misjudged the approach to the same fence and the horse has caught his left knee on the tyres. As the rider has maintained a very good line of sight, and even under these circumstances has not dropped her eyes to the ground, her balance and position remains fairly uninterrupted, despite what the horse is doing underneath her. Had she been looking down at the fence, her upper body would have followed her line of sight and, without doubt, she would have lost her balance and either fallen up the horse's neck or, worse still, onto the ground.

• After some work on her line of sight, the second rider (top right) is now more fully aware of the effects that line of sight has on her balance and position. The improvement is very clear as she tackles a more difficult exercise.

• Using circles and shorter turns while schooling over cross-country fences gives you a chance to concentrate on not allowing the horse to run on along straight lines. Circles and turns also test your balance and control for times when you really need them, such as when turning to a fence or moving away from the fence in any given direction. With the growing number of combinations on curves in competition, this has become a very valuable part of the horse's education. From a schooling point of view, it also creates an equally supple and athletic horse.

Steps

Jumping steps asks questions about balance and confidence. Be aware that many young horses seem to be more suspicious jumping down a step than they are jumping up it. From the rider's point of view, it is essential that you do not get over-enthusiastic and get in front of the movement; alternatively avoid being over-wary and getting behind the movement. Concentrate on keeping your position, balance and line of sight.

Steps down

• For your horse's introduction to steps down, it is important that the step is small enough for him to literally step off the lip without giving himself a fright.

• A young horse's reaction can change very quickly from, "I can't"…

•… to "I'm going as quickly as I can", so you have to be prepared for anything.

• Once your horse is confident and happily popping off a little step, you can progress to something slightly bigger, so encouraging him to jump more forward and freely off the step without losing forward momentum. As demonstrated here, a little pole on the lip of the step usually encourages more of a jump than a slither.

• The rider's line of sight is excellent throughout and her upper body balance is secure. Although her lower leg is a little far back on take-off, it has regained its position and, therefore, security for the landing.

Steps up

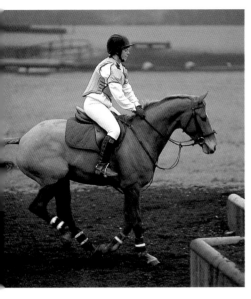  

• When jumping up, young or inexperienced horses can change their balance very quickly, producing a less than comfortable ride. In the first photograph, the horse has dropped behind the rider's leg which props the rider forward. From this slightly backward energy, the horse then over-jumps and jumps out from underneath the rider, resulting in her being left behind and out of balance.

• Through repetition, the horse becomes much more relaxed and confident with the exercise. In this nicely executed jump, the rider is a little in front of the movement.

TROTTING STEPS

With little steps up and down it is best to keep to trot because in canter the horse will tend to just run off the step down or trip going up a small step.

Sunken roads

Once a horse is confident about steps up and down, he can progress to negotiating a small sunken road – a combination of the two questions. Approach with balance and control, in either trot or canter, depending on the horse's stage of training, and maintain this throughout the exercise.

Maintaining your line of sight forward and not looking down into the sunken road, with your lower leg on, will enable the horse to pop down into the sunken road without losing any balance, and take one or two non-jumping strides before jumping up the step unhindered by you. Through the discipline of keeping your line of sight, you will find your balance and position will remain correct. It is important to maintain the horse's energy in the bottom of the sunken road, so that he does not dribble to a stop or trip up the step out.

• This sequence clearly shows the importance of a good line of sight. Without restricting the horse's neck, the rider manages to maintain a contact and therefore her influence over the horse.

• As she canters across the 'road', the rider's balance and line of sight remain correct – she does not tip forward in front of the horse's centre of balance and her lower leg remains underneath her seat. In this position she is able to ride forward effectively to negotiate the step out of the sunken road.

• The fact that the rider has remained in a good balance throughout and is not leaning forward over the horse's shoulders has enabled him to lift his forehand as he pushes off his hindlegs and jumps very correctly out of the sunken road.

Banks

The next stage in training is jumping a simple step up onto a bank followed by a step down, which is the reverse of jumping a sunken road. From this you can advance to jumping up a step onto a bank, taking one or two strides to a small fence on top of the bank and then one or two strides to a drop off the bank. This turns this question into a three-part combination and involves a lot of changes of balance within the horse.

Step onto a bank, jump, and step down

• This young horse jumps confidently through what is a very athletic exercise. He begins by jumping cleanly forward onto the step although the rider is a little in front of the movement, which has allowed her lower leg to slip a little far back. He proceeds fluently to the small fence.

• The rider is not in the best balance and position to encourage the horse through this exercise. However, because the horse is confident and remains generous in his attitude, he continues forward underneath her. Her balance improves in the landing phase (left).

• Finally, there is a step down off the bank, which the horse jumps confidently. The rider has tipped a little forward in front of the movement and her lower leg has slipped back, but her line of sight has remained correct throughout. Shortening the stirrups by two holes would result in her lower leg remaining more secure and her upper body being in better balance.

Ditches and trakehners

Generally, ditches frighten riders more than they frighten horses, although some horses are genuinely suspicious of a hole in the ground. For your first attempt at jumping a ditch, select a small one with plenty of room around it for a horse to make a few mistakes without losing confidence. It is particularly important to introduce young horses to very small ditches on good ground so that they can easily pop from one side to the other. Sometimes a young horse will gain confidence from a lead from a more experienced horse that will jump without hesitation. Some horses will jump a ditch with a pole over it more readily than an open ditch. Your preparatory work in the arena over simulated water trays (p.104) will pay dividends at this point.

In terms of effort, jumping a ditch is more like a non-jumping canter stride for the horse, but it is important that the horse does jump from one side to the other cleanly and does not just canter over the ditch, risking putting a leg into it.

DON'T LOOK DOWN

One of the biggest mistakes when confronted with a ditch is looking down into the ditch (top right). By looking forward and straight ahead you encourage your horse to jump forward and over the ditch. This is seen very clearly in the photograph right, where the pair make a good jump over the obstacle.

Ditches

• Over several attempts, the initial, 'I can't possibly jump that because of the dragon in the bottom' attitude (above) ... will turn into a 'let's get it over with as quickly as possible' one (below).

• But with repetition, you will achieve a more confident, relaxed result.

Trakehners

A trakehner is a ditch with a fence over it. Make the fences small so it is possible to approach in walk if necessary, building up to trot and canter as you and the horse become more confident. This sequence reveals how important it is to expect some initial over reaction to a trakehner-type fence. Again, repetition ensures good progression.

• Initially the horse props a little on sight of the ditch, but he remains forward-thinking and jumps the fence, despite being a little tense. The rider's line of sight was correct on point of take-off but she has not been able to resist the temptation to look down once they are over the ditch.

• Once the pair have jumped the fence a couple of times and gained more confidence, the pole is raised. With the rider's line of sight remaining correct throughout, this young horse is now jumping confidently over a little trakehner. The rider has a correct and effective leg position.

Palisade with a ditch

When jumping any fence incorporating a ditch, it's essential to follow the age-old rule of 'never look into the ditch' (see p.118). It is also important not to allow the horse to look into the ditch, either: keep him in front of the leg, up to the bit and do not weaken your contact. Both you and your horse must be looking in your direction of travel so that you can jump the fence confidently, without allowing the ditch to interrupt your fluency.

• A good confident approach without being too fast. The rider is in good balance and has a correct line of sight.

• The horse takes off confidently and without hesitation, remaining in front of the rider's leg. The rider retains her correct line of sight and good contact, which enables the horse the jump well.

• Even as they are negotiating this obstacle, you can tell from the horse and rider's expression that they are thinking forward to the next fence.

Half coffin

A half coffin consists of a ditch followed by a fence out. As with any challenging combination of jumps, there will inevitably be some tension when the young horse, or inexperienced rider, is first asked to negotiate it, so it is important to work constructively through the exercise several times to build confidence. Pop the ditch first, followed by the 'out' rail, then add in the first set of rails to ride the full coffin combination (opposite). When doing this sort of exercise on an inexperienced horse, it is difficult for the rider to be in balance and relaxed because the horse will be tense. However, the rider must be effective so that the exercise can be repeated several times, which will lead to a more confident and relaxed horse. In this sequence (below), it is easy to see the tension in the rider's face and through her arms and hands.

• Although the horse is travelling forwards underneath the rider, she remains a little stiff in her position and lacks elasticity.

• As a result there is a rather stiff jump from both horse and rider. Note particularly the tight inelastic arm position, which is not truly following the horse's mouth.

Coffin

The difficulty posed by the traditional coffin is that the horse does not see the ditch sitting between the two fences until the point of take-off over the first fence. This sudden sighting of the ditch will often cause a stop or a deterioration of jumping technique through tension over this first part of the obstacle. Therefore, it is vital to approach in an active round and athletic canter that is not too fast. This will provide the impetus to enable the horse to jump athletically over the first fence, even if he is a little suspicious. Once over the first fence it is important to maintain positive energy and keep the roundness in the canter and jump through the rest of the exercise, therefore not quickening and flattening your horse, which would detract from his ability to jump out of the coffin cleanly. This is a classic fence for riders to over-ride.

• This horse is showing a good bold jump over the first element of a coffin and is almost a little too bold at this point. The rider is secure although a little tense.

• The horse judges that he has over-jumped a little and adjusts his length of stride by shortening himself in order to meet the ditch correctly.

• Having shortened, the horse relaxes forward to jump the ditch confidently and in the final photograph (left) exits the coffin cleanly, confidently and correctly. Note the rider's lower leg position throughout the sequence and in particular the fact that her toes are turned out. This is not necessarily a negative point as her lower leg position has remained correct and encouraged the horse to stay forwards and active throughout the exercise.

TRIPLE BAR

A simple triple bar can be ridden positively forwards as the ascending nature of the fence encourages a good, bold, round jump from the horse. Often a ditch will be sited under a triple bar, turning this fence into an elephant trap, which will quite often intimidate a rider more. However, it is ridden in exactly the same way.

Water

Confidence is the key when introducing a horse to water. Take every opportunity to walk, trot and canter in or through water. This is also important for increasing the rider's confidence, as the possibility of getting wet often creates a feeling of negativity in the rider when tackling water obstacles across country.

With a horse that is used to water, try adding an element of fun into this aspect of his training, as simply repeatedly jumping a horse into water can lead to him questioning why he is doing it.

STARTING GENTLY

Initially, a gentle slope into and out of the water is preferable as an introduction to water during a practise session. Even if your horse is usually happy with water, in a strange environment he may be hesitant and should be given time to get used to his surroundings. Before progressing to the next stage, it is important that the horse happily walks, trots and canters through a simple water complex, and copes with the spray that is created by this movement before being asked to jump into the water.

• Once the horse is confident into, through and out of the water, introduce a small step down…

• This pair (top and above) are having a gentle, fun introduction to water. Both are relaxed about the entry and the splashing of the water as they go through. A good grounding will pay off when you encounter more challenging entries into water – don't rush this initial work.

• …and a small step out. Here, both horse and rider are in balance and taking this step up in their stride.

Making progress

Once you are both relaxed about steps in and out of water, it's time to progress to slightly more advanced exercises.

• Here, the balance of both horse and rider is very good and the rider's line of sight is correct as they negotiate a little rail with one or two strides before a step down. Concentration is evident on the rider's face.

• As they jump over the small roller and into the water, the rider is trying hard to maintain her line of sight, despite the strong temptation to look down into the water.

• This has resulted in a little stiffness overall, but with practice and repetition of the exercise, her balance and position will become more relaxed and natural, although discipline will still be required!

BE SENSIBLE ABOUT WATER

• Ensure the footing in the water is secure before taking your horse in.
• Check beforehand that the water is not too deep. It must be well below the horse's knees, in order for him to be able to remain balanced while going through it.
• Always take a dry set of clothing when cross-country schooling (hopefully it won't be needed!)

Roller into water

The next stage in water jumping is to jump a larger roller fence into the water. This progressive work ensures your training develops steadily and that you are building on a solid foundation.

In and out of water and over a jetty fence

When jumping into, out of and back into water maintenance of forward positive energy is doubly important as the drag factor and spray caused by the water can both restrict the horse's movement and distort his vision. The change in the horse's balance through this collection of obstacles also alters the rider's balance. Jumping through this sort of exercise can feel a little like being on a roller coaster until you have perfected the various changes in balance. When executed correctly, however, it can be exhilarating and great fun for horse and rider!

• The horse is confident and able to deal with the question being asked of her – a result of good early training. The rider is a little apprehensive and is looking down a little but corrects this as the pair move on.

• Although somewhat tense, the rider has not restricted the horse and it is possible to see the confidence blossoming in this partnership.

• Through repetition of the exercise, the rider will become more confident and as relaxed as the horse, and therefore lose any tension caused by inevitable apprehension.

• Horse and rider jump down a step, canter through the water, jump out of the water onto a jetty and immediately bounce over a little roller back into the water. You can see that the horse remains fluently forward, in front of the rider's leg, carrying the rider in a good balance. Note the rider's line of sight throughout this exercise, and the athleticism in the horse.

Narrow brush, step down and log

Like the step down to the arrowhead (pp.126–7), an exercise like this, involving a scalloped narrow brush fence, then a step down and then a hanging log, is a test of straightness and balance. You can see how tempting it is for the rider to look down with their eyes even when maintaining a good position with their head.

• As they clear the first obstacle, the rider has looked down and allowed the horse to jump a little through his right shoulder.

• The horse jumps very correctly down the step (top and above) while remaining straight. Although the rider's balance is a little wobbly, the horse remains straight underneath her.

• She quickly corrects her line of sight, as well as using her right leg to straighten the horse. Because she has used her leg rather than relying too much on her hands, the horse's head and neck have remained straight during this correction, which is very important.

• With a good line of sight, and maintenance of balance and rhythm, the horse negotiates the hanging log after the step.

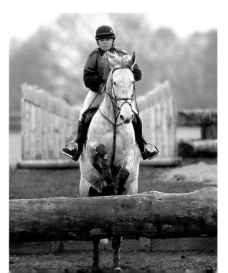

TIPS FOR ACCURACY FENCES

• Ensure both rein contacts are equal and the horse's neck is straight.

• Have an equal pressure against the horse's sides in both legs.

• If you keep your line of sight correct you will find that your balance and position remain correct throughout the exercise.

• If your horse drifts left or right, remember to correct with your legs and not the contact. Using too strong a rein will create bend and encourage the horse to drift even more through its shoulder.

In reverse – log, step up and narrow brush

By jumping this combination of fences in reverse, the difficulty is increased as the trickiest part of the combination – the narrow brush – comes at the end. The key to success is to maintain the power through the whole exercise and think about riding this combination as a log to two steps up.

• At the step, the rider's weight has slipped a little to the right; the horse drifts left as the rider's left leg is not on sufficiently.

• From behind imperfections are starkly visible: the rider has more weight in her right stirrup and her left leg has slipped a little too far back. However, the horse has remained straight.

• But the rider manages to regain control and has closed her left leg to straighten the horse to jump the narrow brush.

• As they clear the log, the rider is a little in front of the movement in anticipation of jumping up the step, but this does not restrict the horse, and she jumps confidently.

Log and drop

This log and drop is approached at the top of a hill, making it seem more imposing. Until you get to the very edge of the drop, you feel like you are about to drop off a cliff. However, it is a novice fence and does not demand that much of a confident and well-trained horse and rider.

• You can see how the rider's line of sight is down to the log, which makes the horse suspicious. This leads to him not thinking forwards and culminates in a refusal.

• Once the rider has improved her line of sight and her balance, the horse clears the log and drop easily. It is human nature to look at the point of take-off or point of landing. Discipline is required to ensure that you look straight ahead and maintain your balance.

Steps

When jumping down a series of related steps, it is important to realize that many horses will gain impetus and length of stride as they progress, and therefore lose co-ordination. It is vital to have control over your horse through your lower leg, your back and shoulders, and an elastic rein contact to ensure he stays together and doesn't land on his nose (literally!) at the bottom of the steps.

Angled steps

This question is a sequence of steps, each with a 1m (3ft) drop. To add further difficulty, they are on varying distances and are angled. As they are angled, it is to be expected that the horse will tend to drift as he negotiates each step. However, balanced correct riding, with both legs into both reins and a secure upper body position, will encourage the horse to remain as straight as possible while he is learning and absolutely straight when fully trained.

• Horse and rider start well, coming down the first step straight. They have successfully navigated the hardest part, as from the top to the bottom it looks a long way down for both the horse and rider.

• Coming off the second step, the horse is now falling into his left shoulder. The rider is trying to keep him straight, but she could be a little more effective with her left leg.

• As they negotiate the third step, which is angled in the opposite direction…

• … the horse naturally starts to drift right, encouraged by the step's angle.

• Having drifted both ways, the horse then becomes straight for the last step, thanks to the rider keeping an even contact through the reins and her legs.

Water

As the horses are more advanced in this clinic, we tackle a couple of more imposing water complexes, which comprise fences of bigger dimensions – height and width – and bigger drops into water. These more demanding fences must only be presented to an established and confident horse across country.

Novice combination water jump

This is a novice question showing a combination of a small boathouse fence, then two non-jumping strides, a step into water and three strides across the water to a step out.

• The horse jumps confidently over the first element, which is a small boathouse fence. The rider is in a good balance.

• Maintaining this correct position has allowed the rider to ride positively forwards to the contact with the horse remaining in front of her legs.

• While not dropping the contact, the rider allows the horse to lengthen his neck to jump into the water confidently.

• She then maintains a consistent contact, without pulling back, enabling the horse to lift his forehand and canter 'uphill' through the water.

• As he proceeds, the horse becomes a little bold and in order to stop him running through the water and tripping up the step, the rider takes steps to control the speed.

• Having regained control, the rider can again relax and soften the contact allowing the horse to jump correctly out of the water. It is important to make any adjustments to speed quickly and effectively as they arise in this situation, so that you can relax and allow the horse more freedom sooner and therefore enable him to jump out of the obstacle unrestricted.

Intermediate combination water jump

The question posed with this intermediate fence (below) is similar to the novice combination in the previous sequence (left). It entails a larger boathouse and one non-jumping stride to a step into water. This is a more difficult exercise due to the bigger dimensions of the fence and the closer proximity to the water.

Log drop into water

This intermediate fence (right) comprises two logs on top of each other with a drop into water. It is a perfect illustration of the rider's line of sight controlling her balance and position while jumping what can often be a very unbalancing type of obstacle.

• Although the horse makes a bold confident jump, as he lands he has a slightly wary expression on his face. However, due to the rider's confident approach, correct leg to rein connection and forward line of sight, he is encouraged, which guarantees a confident and balanced jump into the water.

• The rider allows the horse to relax his head and neck while jumping down into the water but maintains contact upon landing as too much freedom of rein can cause a horse to stumble and peck. A horse can also lose his balance when the drag of the water slows him down, so the security of the contact is vital. The importance of the rider's good line of sight and the balance of horse and rider cannot be overstated.

Index